Computer Science

Reflections on the Field,
Reflections from the Field

Committee on the Fundamentals of Computer
Science: Challenges and Opportunities

Computer Science and Telecommunications Board

NATIONAL RESEARCH COUNCIL
OF THE NATIONAL ACADEMIES

THE NATIONAL ACADEMIES PRESS
Washington, D.C.
www.nap.edu

THE NATIONAL ACADEMIES PRESS 500 Fifth Street, N.W. Washington, DC 20001

NOTICE: The project that is the subject of this report was approved by the Governing Board of the National Research Council, whose members are drawn from the councils of the National Academy of Sciences, the National Academy of Engineering, and the Institute of Medicine. The members of the committee responsible for the report were chosen for their special competences and with regard for appropriate balance.

Support for this project was provided by the National Science Foundation under grant No. CCR-9981754. Any opinions, findings, conclusions, or recommendations expressed in this publication are those of the authors and do not necessarily reflect the views of the sponsor.

International Standard Book Number 0-309-09301-5 (Book)
International Standard Book Number 0-309-54529-3 (PDF)

Copies of this report are available from the National Academies Press, 500 Fifth Street, N.W., Lockbox 285, Washington, DC 20055; (800) 624-6242 or (202) 334-3313 in the Washington metropolitan area; Internet, http://www.nap.edu.

THE NATIONAL ACADEMIES
Advisers to the Nation on Science, Engineering, and Medicine

The **National Academy of Sciences** is a private, nonprofit, self-perpetuating society of distinguished scholars engaged in scientific and engineering research, dedicated to the furtherance of science and technology and to their use for the general welfare. Upon the authority of the charter granted to it by the Congress in 1863, the Academy has a mandate that requires it to advise the federal government on scientific and technical matters. Dr. Bruce M. Alberts is president of the National Academy of Sciences.

The **National Academy of Engineering** was established in 1964, under the charter of the National Academy of Sciences, as a parallel organization of outstanding engineers. It is autonomous in its administration and in the selection of its members, sharing with the National Academy of Sciences the responsibility for advising the federal government. The National Academy of Engineering also sponsors engineering programs aimed at meeting national needs, encourages education and research, and recognizes the superior achievements of engineers. Dr. Wm. A. Wulf is president of the National Academy of Engineering.

The **Institute of Medicine** was established in 1970 by the National Academy of Sciences to secure the services of eminent members of appropriate professions in the examination of policy matters pertaining to the health of the public. The Institute acts under the responsibility given to the National Academy of Sciences by its congressional charter to be an adviser to the federal government and, upon its own initiative, to identify issues of medical care, research, and education. Dr. Harvey V. Fineberg is president of the Institute of Medicine.

The **National Research Council** was organized by the National Academy of Sciences in 1916 to associate the broad community of science and technology with the Academy's purposes of furthering knowledge and advising the federal government. Functioning in accordance with general policies determined by the Academy, the Council has become the principal operating agency of both the National Academy of Sciences and the National Academy of Engineering in providing services to the government, the public, and the scientific and engineering communities. The Council is administered jointly by both Academies and the Institute of Medicine. Dr. Bruce M. Alberts and Dr. Wm. A. Wulf are chair and vice chair, respectively, of the National Research Council.

www.national-academies.org

Preface

The blossoming of computer science (CS) research is evident in the information technology that has migrated from a specialized tool confined to the laboratory or corporate back office to a ubiquitous presence in machines and devices that now figure in the lives of virtually every individual. This widespread diffusion of information technology can obscure the nature of computer science research underlying the IT—from the perspective of many outside the field, computer science is seen not as a basic area of systematic inquiry but as a tool to support other endeavors.

Mindful of these issues, the National Science Foundation's Computer and Information Science and Engineering Directorate asked the Computer Science and Telecommunications Board of the National Academies to conduct a study that would improve understanding of CS research among the scientific community at large, policymakers, and the general public. By describing in accessible form the field's intellectual character and by conveying a sense of its vibrancy through a set of examples, the committee also aims to prepare readers for what the future might hold and inspire CS researchers to help create it.

This volume, the product of that study, is divided into two parts that contain nine chapters.

The volume's prelude, "Emily Shops at VirtualEmporia.com," takes a now-familiar use of computing—shopping online—and illustrates how CS research has made this seemingly simple activity possible.

Part One—Chapter 1, "The Essential Character of Computer Science"—offers the committee's concise characterization of CS research. Like CS researchers more generally, the committee members evince a wide range of perspectives that mirror the broad reach of computation into the very fabric of our intellectual and physical lives. Recognizing the richness and diversity of the field, the committee expressly decided not to provide either a comprehensive list of research topics or a taxonomy of research areas, nor to develop criteria for what research is inside and outside of CS. Instead, the committee's approach is to describe some key ideas that lie at the core of CS but not to define boundaries.

Part Two—Chapters 2 through 9—comprises two dozen essays written by committee members, participants in a June 6-7, 2001, symposium organized by the committee, and other invited authors. The essays describe several aspects of CS research and some of the results from the perspectives of their authors. By providing this diverse set of views on CS research, the committee aims to express some of the spark that motivates and excites CS researchers. The essays have a deliberately historical focus, for three reasons: (1) as described above, the committee decided not to present a research agenda, either explicit or implicit; (2) other publications look at current, hot topics in CS and these tend, in any case, to become dated quickly; and (3) results that have proven durable best illustrate the strengths of CS.

The prelude and Part One are intended to be accessible to all readers (as are many of the essays). But because this report is also intended to reach scientists and engineers from a variety of disciplines, a few of the essays do presume some familiarity with some technical concepts.

The committee would like to thank all of the participants in the June 2001 symposium; presentations and informal discussions at that event provided important input to the committee. Julie Sussman, PPA, provided a number of helpful suggestions concerning the manuscript. The reviewers listed below provided many valuable suggestions for improvement.

Mary Shaw, *Chair*
Committee on the Fundamentals of Computer Science:
Challenges and Opportunities

Acknowledgment of Reviewers

This report has been reviewed in draft form by individuals chosen for their diverse perspectives and technical expertise, in accordance with procedures approved by the National Research Council's Report Review Committee. The purpose of this independent review is to provide candid and critical comments that will assist the institution in making its published report as sound as possible and to ensure that the report meets institutional standards for objectivity, evidence, and responsiveness to the study charge. The review comments and draft manuscript remain confidential to protect the integrity of the deliberative process. We wish to thank the following individuals for their review of this report:

David D. Clark, Massachusetts Institute of Technology
Robert L. Constable, Cornell University
Ronald Fedkiw, Stanford University
Joan Feigenbaum, Yale University
Juris Hartmanis, Cornell University
James Jay Horning, Intertrust
Anna R. Karlin, University of Washington
Richard Karp, University of California, Berkeley
Wendy A. Kellog, IBM Research
Monica S. Lam, Stanford University
Butler W. Lampson, Microsoft Research
Fred B. Schneider, Cornell University
Lynn Andrea Stein, Olin College

Gerald Jay Sussman, Massachusetts Institute of Technology
Thomas N. Theis, IBM T.J. Watson Research Center
Jeanette M. Wing, Carnegie Mellon University
Margaret H. Wright, New York University

Although the reviewers listed above provided many constructive comments and suggestions, they were not asked to endorse the conclusions or recommendations nor did they see the final draft of the report before its release. The review of this report was overseen by Lawrence Snyder, University of Washington. Appointed by the National Research Council, he was responsible for making certain that an independent examination of this report was carried out in accordance with institutional procedures and that all review comments were carefully considered. Responsibility for the final content of this report rests entirely with the authoring committee and the institution.

Contents

Prelude

Emily Shops at VirtualEmporia.com

Just a decade ago, the Internet was the domain of specialists and technology aficionados, requiring knowledge of file systems, format compatibilities, and operating system commands. Even the more user-friendly systems such as e-mail and net news principally served relatively small communities of technically savvy people.

Until recently, the Internet, the World Wide Web, and e-commerce all would have seemed akin to magic to all but the most tech-savvy. Yet despite today's widespread acceptance of and familiarity with computer capabilities, the details of how commonly used computer systems work remains a mystery for non-specialists. It is not magic, of course, that is at work. Nor did today's system arise as a result of a direct evolution of previous technology.

Like many radical innovations, e-commerce, for one, was not planned or even anticipated by those involved in either research or commerce. Rather, it evolved from a series of technical results that were pursued with other motivations—such as sharing computer resources or scientific information among researchers. Examining the scientific roots of e-commerce shows how research pursued for its own sake can enable important, often unanticipated capabilities.

We take as our example a hypothetical online retailer, VirtualEmporia.com, and reveal some of the magic—that is, the research foundations—behind the now-simple operation of ordering a book online. Thus it is possible to identify some of the computer science (CS) research that enables retailing online and to provide pointers to discussions of that research later in this volume. Also noted are some of the ways that a virtual store can provide an intellectual boost over a conventional store through its capabilities for searching and indexing, exchanging information among customers, and providing an enormous catalog of items.

Emily is planning to take a trip next week and she's looking for something to read on the airplane. In the past, she would have gone to a bookstore during business hours and browsed through the shelves to select a book from the limited stock at hand. Today, Emily has the option of sitting down at a computer, at any time of the day or night, to select and buy a book or many other types of products.

Although shopping online is now a routine experience for millions, its familiarity and simplicity mask the sophisticated events behind the scenes. Indeed, what Emily does in the next 5 minutes would have been impossible without many discoveries and inventions from computer science.

Emily's Computer

Emily's family, like more than half of the households in the United States, owns a personal computer and related software. Her garden-variety home PC, available for roughly $600, is able to run much more sophisticated programs—and run them much faster—than the first computer her employer bought only 20 years ago. Indeed, the very idea of a home computer, outside the professional or aficionado market, is only about 20 years old.

If Emily were to pause and consider the functionality available to her, she might marvel that no other machine is as flexible, general-purpose, or malleable as a computer. The idea that machines can be adapted to completely new situations for which they were not originally designed usually borders on the farcical. Emily's pencil will not also serve as a stapler if the need arises. Computers, though, are

The cost of computing power has decreased dramatically. A typical 2003 home PC, which had a 2.66 GHz system clock, 256 Mb of RAM, and a 40 Gb hard drive, outperformed the IBM/XT PC, released in 1983, which had a 4.77 MHz system clock, 640 Kb of RAM, and a 10 Mb hard drive, by a factor of roughly 500—at one-tenth the cost. Hill (in Chapter 2) describes the phenomenon of exponential growth in computing power, and he shows how computer science research strives to design computers that sustain this remarkable rate of improvement in the cost/performance ratio of computers.

Emily's computer and software are remarkable not only for their low cost but also for their high complexity. The hardware comprises billions of transistors, and the software installed on the computer is defined by tens of millions of lines of code; hundreds of millions of lines of additional software is available. The capability of the computer is built up from these tiny elements.

Shaw (in Chapter 4) describes how abstraction hides the complex and often-messy details of a piece of hardware or software in favor of a simpler, more focused view of the aspects of immediate universal symbol manipulators covering the entire gamut of information processing. The right software transforms a computer from a Web browser to a home accountant to a photo editor to a jukebox to a mailbox to a game, virtually at your whim.

Although Emily's computer arrived at her home with a large amount of software pre-installed (including the Web browser that Emily uses to shop at VirtualEmporia.com), it can also run tens of thousands of additional programs. Of course, Emily will actually use only a small fraction of those programs, but she has enormous variety to choose from. These programs potentially enable Emily to use her computer for many different tasks, ranging from applications inconceivable before we had computers—such as e-mail, online messenger services, or chat rooms—to computer-based enhancements to more traditional tasks like creating and typesetting documents, organizing a business, or tracking investments.

relevance. This makes it possible to build enormously complex systems out of a tower of abstractions, one layer at a time. Systematic research on algorithms and data structures was also necessary to build such complex software and hardware systems.

Nothing else—aside from a person—is a universal machine that can be taught or programmed to accomplish a very wide range of new tasks. Kleinberg and Papadimitriou (in Chapter 2) show how the idea of universality rests on the notion of the universal Turing machine and the Church-Turing hypothesis about the universality of computers.

The capabilities of Emily's computer can be improved as current programs are improved, and even not-yet-conceived capabilities can be added as new programs are written. Software tools—programs that manipulate and transform other programs—make it possible to create new applications. The most important of these tools are the programming languages that provide the grammar, syntax, and semantics programmers use to convey their ideas to computers. A wide range of programming languages and tools are available today and new languages and tools are the subject of computer science research. See Aho and Larus in Chapter 4.

Human-computer interaction research has led to improved user interfaces that make it easier for people to work with this software. Foley (in Chapter 8) discusses how research on user interfaces made spreadsheet software easier to use.

Ullman (in Chapter 8) describes the computer science research that led to today's word processors.

Foley (in Chapter 8) describes how a variety of CS research results made possible another kind of computer program, the spreadsheet.

Visiting VirtualEmporia.com

Equally remarkably, Emily's computer is easily connected to the Internet. This allows her to obtain information from billions of Web pages, communicate with others using e-mail or chat programs, or use a myriad of other Internet-delivered services. Once she is online and has opened a Web browser, she can visit VirtualEmporia.com simply by typing "http:// www.VirtualEmporia.com" or selecting a bookmark. Her computer translates the name of the destination site into an Internet address and sends a message across the Internet to VirtualEmporia, asking for a Web page, which contains links to the rest of VirtualEmporia's network.

The Internet, which made data exchange among distant computers fast, easy, and commonplace, marked a striking change in the use of computers. The Internet also represented a striking change in how communications networks were designed. The Internet is a distributed, fault-tolerant system for communicating among computers. Its design specifies very little about the form or content of data—that aspect is left to the applications and systems enabled by the Internet's packet-data-transport mechanisms (see Peterson and Clark in Chapter 7). With few changes to its design or implementation, the Internet grew from approximately 300,000 interconnected machines (hosts) in 1990 to over 170 million hosts in 2003.[1]

Although the Internet was originally constructed to allow researchers to share data and remotely access expensive computers, users of the early Internet quickly made e-mail the most popular application, and it remains the most common use of the Internet today. Today, the Internet is opening up many new avenues for communication among people (see Bruckman in Chapter 7).

The Internet's success derives in large part from the fact that it provides effective abstractions to enable computers throughout the world to find each other and exchange data. Here, Emily's browser and VirtualEmporia.com's Web site use a communication protocol called http that is built on top of the Internet.

The World Wide Web, another of the many uses of the Internet, owes its origins in part to earlier computer science research on hypertext, which provides a way of navigating among linked documents.

---

[1]Internet Systems Consortium (ISC), 2004, *"Internet Domain Survey,"* ISC, Redwood City, Calif., January. Available online at http://www.isc.org/ds/.

Shopping

When Emily visits VirtualEmporia.com's Web site, VirtualEmporia.com recognizes Emily as an established customer. It retrieves her records and produces a customized home page, based on her past shopping habits, that suggests a few items she might want to buy. As she navigates through the site, the pages she views are also customized. VirtualEmporia.com suggests new books that might interest her, based on previous items she has purchased or searched for. In addition, when she looks at items or adds them to her shopping cart, VirtualEmporia shows her more items that customers with similar shopping interests have selected.

Research on collaborative filtering led to machine-learning algorithms that correlate a new shopper's interests with those of other shoppers in the database, so that data from the entire shopping community can be used to learn Emily's likely interests. Mitchell (in Chapter 6) discusses some other applications of machine learning.

Emily can also refine her choices by reading reviews on the VirtualEmporia site, including reviews published by recognized critics and comments from other customers—which she takes more or less seriously depending on the credibility ratings these comments have accumulated.

Computer science research on reputation systems allows VirtualEmporia to provide some indications of how much trust one should place in opinions contributed by strangers.

Emily can browse through the items for sale or search the database of available products. Emily first enters a search request by author's name. She receives a response in a second or less, even though VirtualEmporia's database contains information about millions of books and other items for sale, has tens of millions of registered customers, and may

Like many modern organizations such as airlines, banks, and governments, VirtualEmporia could not exist in its current form without database systems. Gray (in Chapter 5) describes the research that led to the relational model for databases and modern database systems. Building on this discovery, computer scientists have developed a rich collection of representations and algorithms for manipulating data; this makes it feasible to store, index, search, update, and sort billions of records in reasonable amounts receive queries from hundreds of users each second. Emily does not find the book (she doesn't quite remember the author's name), but she does remember the name of a character in the book, which she uses in a full-content search to locate the desired book.

The online setting enables business partnerships that were previously difficult or impossible. VirtualEmporia also allows Emily to consider offerings from multiple booksellers, including not only a large seller who can provide almost all books currently in print, but also numerous used-book sellers, both companies and individuals. When Emily searches for a book, she not only gets information about how to order that book and other editions of that book but also the opportunity to buy a used copy from the many booksellers and individuals who list books at VirtualEmporia.

Paying for the Book

After some browsing and searching, Emily finds the books she wants and goes to the checkout page, which asks for a credit card number.

Emily's credit card information is automatically encrypted by her Web browser before it is sent over the Internet, making it harder for an unauthorized person to obtain it, even though the information is

of time, and to ensure their integrity in the face of overlapping queries and updates.

The ability to store and rapidly process such enormous and growing volumes of information also depends on work leading to the ever-increasing performance of computers (see Hill in Chapter 2).

Sudan (in Chapter 7) explains how public-key encryption, a technology stemming from cryptology research, makes it possible for a business such as VirtualEmporia.com to engage in secure communications with millions of individuals.

traveling across the Internet's shared infrastructure and could potentially be processed by tens or hundreds of computers along the path between her computer and VirtualEmporia.

Shipping the Book

VirtualEmporia's shipping system makes use of software algorithms to decide which warehouse to use for the books Emily has ordered, whether the books will all be shipped in one package or separately to help speed the books to Emily, which shipper to select, and so forth.

Even though the books are physical objects that traveled by airplane and truck, their rapid journey is assisted by the shipper's computerized logistics systems that inventory, schedule, and track the books' journey. These systems also make it possible for Emily to track a package through a Web site and receive updates on when she can expect the package to arrive.

Conclusion

Emily's books will arrive at her home a few days later. Impatiently awaiting her purchase, Emily starts to wonder why the book even had to be a physical object: why couldn't it just be delivered as a digital object, transmitted over the Internet? Indeed, computer science research has already

Information encoded with a public key can be decrypted only with the corresponding private key. VirtualEmporia.com publishes its public key, which anyone can use to encrypt information and securely send it to VirtualEmporia.com. Only VirtualEmporia.com, however, knows the private key for decrypting these messages. This technique can be applied both ways: software on Emily's computer can use the secure channel to VirtualEmporia.com to create a new one in the reverse direction (from VirtualEmporia.com to Emily). Therefore confidential two-way communication can proceed, protected from prying eyes.

A special secure version of the World Wide Web communication protocol provides a layer of abstraction that makes it possible for Emily to use secure communication without knowing about the details.

Inventory management and routing are both examples of activities involving information manipulation. Before computer science, these processes could be accomplished only by hand. Computerized inventory and routing algorithms have made express shipping much more efficient. The result has been a reduction of both the costs and the elapsed time for delivery.

Like shopping, package tracking depends on database systems. It also depends on wireless communications from the delivery people who carry portable wireless devices. These devices owe their origins to research on wireless networks and low-power devices.

provided many of the necessary foundations of electronic books and has built prototypes of all the basic components. Electronic books have just entered the commercial marketplace and may become more commonplace once inexpensive and practical book-like reading devices become available.

An "early adopter," Emily decides she wants something to read right away. She goes to VirtualEmporia's e-books department, orders and downloads a book, and starts reading it within minutes.

Perhaps what is most remarkable about Emily's shopping experience is that it's so commonplace today (and electronic books may become commonplace just over the horizon), while just 10 years ago it seemed far-fetched—even as the computer science groundwork was being laid. What other stories, which may seem fantastic today even as computer science research is laying their foundations, will we come to label mundane 10 and 20 years from now?

Part One

The Essential Character of Computer Science

.

1

The Essential Character of
Computer Science

C omputer science began to emerge as a distinct field in the 1940s
and 1950s with the development of the first electronic digital computers. Their creation reflected several coincident factors—the
development of computational theory in the 1930s and 1940s, the existence of compelling computational applications (starting with wartime
needs such as codebreaking and the calculation of artillery trajectories),
and the availability of electronic components with which to implement
computers for those applications. A number of mathematicians, engineers,
economists, and physicists turned their attention to mastering and
enhancing the capabilities of this novel tool. But computers proved so
powerful and absorbing, so interesting and open-ended, and so uniquely
challenging that many of these people realized, a decade or so later, that
they had in fact left their original disciplines and were pioneering a
new field.

Computer science embraces questions ranging from the properties of
electronic devices to the character of human understanding, from individual designed components to globally distributed systems, and from
the purely theoretical to the highly pragmatic. Its research methods are
correspondingly inclusive, spanning theory, analysis, experimentation,
construction, and modeling. Computer science encompasses basic research
that seeks fundamental understanding of computational phenomena, as
well as applied research. The two are often coupled; grappling with practical problems inspires fundamental insights. Given this breadth and
diversity, the discussion that follows does not aim to explicitly or compre-

hensively define computer science or to catalog all of the research areas. (Indeed, such an effort would inevitably bog down in classifying sub-disciplines of the field and declaring interdisciplinary activities as "in" or "out.") Instead, the approach is to indicate and illustrate the essential character of the field through a sampling of representative topics.

WHAT IS COMPUTER SCIENCE?

Computer science is the study of computers and what they can do—the inherent powers and limitations of abstract computers, the design and character-istics of real computers, and the innumerable applications of computers to solv-ing problems. Computer scientists seek to understand how to represent and to reason about processes and information. They create languages for representing these phenomena and develop methods for analyzing and creating the phenomena. They create abstractions, including abstractions that are themselves used to compose, manipulate, and represent other abstractions. They study the symbolic representation, implementation, manipulation, and communication of information. They create, study, experiment on, and improve real-world computational and information systems—the working hardware and software *artifacts* that embody the computing capabilities. They develop models, methods, and technologies to help design, realize, and operate these artifacts. They amplify human intellect through the automation of rote tasks and construction of new capabilities.

Computer hardware and software have been central to computer sci-ence since its origins. However, computer science also encompasses the study and more general application of principles and theories rooted in or motivated by hardware and software phenomena. Computer science has thus come to encompass topics once distinctly part of other disciplines, such as mathematics, originally motivated by computing and conceptual questions of information-handling tasks such as natural-language pro-cessing. Computer science research is often intimately intertwined with application, as the need to solve practical problems drives new theoretical breakthroughs.

The accompanying essays in this volume elaborate on some impor-tant examples of the results of computer science research. These include:

- The Universal Turing Machine and the Church-Turing thesis, which provide a theoretical underpinning for understanding computing (see Kleinberg and Papadimitriou in Chapter 2);
- Computer programs that achieve, exceed, or augment human per-formance levels in challenging intellectual tasks (see Koller and Bierman and also Mitchell in Chapter 6);

- The theory of algorithms—formal expressions of procedures—which separate algorithmic behavior from the specific code that implements it (see Kleinberg and Papadimitriou in Chapter 2);
- Programming languages, which are notations specifically designed to represent computational processes, or how things happen (see Aho and Larus in Chapter 4);
- The relational model of data, which provided a systematic way to express complex associations among data and revolutionized the database industry and provided the basis for nearly all business computing (see Gray in Chapter 5);
- The Internet, a reliable system created from unreliable parts that defines a simple, general-purpose abstraction of a packet network on which a wide range of applications can be constructed (see Peterson and Clark in Chapter 7);
- Simulation, which permits the study and visualization of both natural and man-made phenomena (see Fedkiw in Chapter 3); and
- Software systems that allow non-experts to use computers (see Foley and also Ullman in Chapter 8).

Computer science's striking research advances have touched our lives in profound ways as we work, learn, play, and communicate. Even though computer science is a relatively young field, born only within the past seven decades, the pace of innovation in it has been extraordinary. Once esoteric, expensive, and reserved for specialized tasks, computers are now seemingly everywhere. Applications and technologies that are now fixtures in many people's lives and work (such as office automation, e-commerce, and search engines) were nonexistent or barely visible just a decade ago. The personal computer itself was first introduced less then three decades ago, yet most office workers are now assigned a PC as a matter of course, and roughly half of all households in the United States own at least one. Computers are central to the daily operations of banks, brokerage houses, airlines, telephone systems, and supermarkets. Even more computers lurk hidden inside handheld cell phones, personal digital assistants, and automobiles; for example, a typical midmarket automobile contains a network and dozens of processors. As the size and cost of computer hardware shrink, computers will continue to proliferate even more widely (see Hill in Chapter 2). All these computers have provided society with tremendous social and economic benefits even as they pose new challenges for public policy and social organizations.

Advances in computer science have also led to fundamental changes in many scientific and engineering disciplines, enabling, for example, complex numerical calculations that would simply be infeasible if attempted by hand. Computer science has provided highly useful tools for controlling experiments, collecting, exchanging, and analyzing data, modeling and simulation, and for sharing scientific information. Indeed, finding the right data structure or algorithm can revolutionize the way in which a scientist thinks about a problem. For example, computer science algorithms made it possible to put together a vast amount of data from sequencing machines when the human genome was sequenced. In recent years, reflecting information's central importance in scholarly work and science, computing has also taken on new importance in many other disciplines as well; Ayers (in Chapter 5), for example, discusses ways in which historians are using computing. Computer science's computational paradigm has also shaped new modes of inquiry in other fields, such as genomics and related areas of biology.

One driver of computer science innovation is the doubling of hardware performance that we have seen roughly every $1\frac{1}{2}$ to 2 years (see Hill in Chapter 2). Another is the invention of myriad new applications of computers, whose creation is made possible by the tremendous flexibility of software. Computer applications are largely limited only by human imagination, although there are fundamental limits on what is computable and there are significant engineering challenges in building complex systems.

This volume explores computer science research, emphasizing how research leads both to deeper understanding of computation and to numerous practical applications. Many others have celebrated the accomplishments of computer science or offered predictions about future directions.[1] The emphasis in this volume is on why and how computer scientists do their research.

Part Two of this volume consists of a set of individually authored essays that provide a sampling of perspectives on several areas of computer science research. These are intended to exemplify some of the observations made in this chapter and illustrate some of the flavor of computer science.

This chapter broadly considers the essential character of computer science (what does computer science investigate, design, and create?), and its methods and modes of research (how do computer scientists

---

[1]For example, Cathy A. Lazere and Dennis Elliott Shasha, 1998, *Out of Their Minds: The Lives and Discoveries of 15 Great Computer Scientists*, Copernicus Books, celebrates accomplishments of the field. Works describing future research directions include CSTB, NRC, 1992, *Computing the Future*, National Academy Press; Peter J. Denning and Robert M. Metcalfe, eds., 1997, *Beyond Calculation: The Next Fifty Years of Computing*, Springer-Verlag; and Peter J. Denning, ed., 1999, *Talking Back to the Machine: Computers and Human Aspiration*, Springer-Verlag. Bruce W. Arden, 1980, *What Can be Automated: The Computer Science and Engineering Research Study*, MIT Press, was an attempt to comprehensively survey the field.

approach problems? what methods do they use? and what types of results emerge?). The discussion below elucidates seven major themes without attempting to fully enumerate all the research subfields within computer science, to prescribe a research agenda, or to define the boundaries of computer science.

SALIENT CHARACTERISTICS OF
COMPUTER SCIENCE RESEARCH

The character of a research field arises from the phenomena it seeks to understand and manipulate together with the types of questions the discipline seeks to answer about these phenomena. This section identifies phenomena and intellectual challenges central to computer science, describing the key ideas and the identifying work that has helped to develop those ideas. These broad themes (summarized in Box 1.1), more timeless than a comprehensive inventory of current topics would be, portray core ideas that computer science is concerned with.

Computer Science Research Involves Symbols and
Their Manipulation

Two of the fundamental techniques of computer science research are the manipulation of discrete information and symbolic representation. Some information is inherently discrete, such as money. Discrete approximation enables every kind of information to be represented within the computer by a sequence of bits (choices of 0 or 1) or the often more

---

BOX 1.1
Salient Characteristics of Computer Science Research

• Computer science research involves symbols and their manipulation.
• Computer science research involves the creation and manipulation of abstractions.
• Computer science research creates and studies algorithms.
• Computer science research creates artificial constructs, notably unlimited by physical laws.
• Computer science research exploits and addresses exponential growth.
• Computer science research seeks the fundamental limits on what can be computed.
• Computer science research often focuses on the complex, analytic, rational action that is associated with human intelligence.

convenient bytes (sequences of 8 bits, representing characters such as letters) to which the proper interpretation is applied. A digital image of any one of Van Gogh's paintings of sunflowers (call it *Sunflowers*, for short) divides the continuous painted canvas into many small rectangular regions called pixels and gives the (approximate) color at each of these. The collection of pixels can, in turn, be thought of as a sequence of bits. Bit sequences, being a "digital" or discrete-valued representation, cannot fully represent precise, real-valued or "analog" information (e.g., the precise amount of yellow in a sunflower). Practically, though, this apparent limitation can be overcome by using a sufficiently large enough number of bits, to, for example, represent the analog information as precisely as the eye can see or the ear can hear.

This sequence of bits can be processed in one way so that a person can see the *Sunflowers* image on a display or processed another way for a printer to print an image. This sequence of bits could be sent in an e-mail message to a friend or posted to a Web page. In principle, the same sequence of bits could be passed to an audio interpreter; however, the audio produced by *Sunflowers* would not sound very good, since this bit sequence is unlikely to represent anything reasonable in the symbol system used by the audio player. *Sunflowers* could be executed as a program on the computer, since programs are themselves bit strings; again, however, the result will probably not produce anything meaningful, since it is unlikely the painting's representation is a sequence that will do something useful.

More subtle than discrete approximation, yet more powerful, is the technique of symbolic representation. Here the underlying bits are used to represent symbols in some notation, and that notation is used to represent information in a way that permits analysis and further processing. For example:

- For analysis of differences among sunflowers or between sunflowers and marigolds, flowers could be described in terms of their genetic code.
- For graphical animation, a sunflower might be represented by a description of the color and shape of its parts together with how they are connected to each other.
- To denote different varieties, sunflowers might be represented by a set of symbols consisting of words in English.

The right symbol systems, properly interpreted, allow one to write programs that represent and manipulate sounds or images, that simulate physical phenomena, and even that create artificial systems without an analog in nature.

Several of the essays in this volume deal with symbolic representation. The essay by Kleinberg and Papadimitriou in Chapter 2 discusses the formal representation of computation itself as symbol strings. Lesk in Chapter 5 mentions many of the important kinds of representations being stored in computers as "digital libraries."

Computer Science Research Involves the Creation and Manipulation of Abstraction

Computer science often involves formulating and manipulating abstractions, which are coordinated sets of definitions that capture different aspects of a particular entity—from broad concept to its detailed representation in bits—and the relations through which some of the definitions refine others or provide additional concepts to help realize others.

One aspect of abstraction is that sequences of bits take on specific useful interpretations that make sense only in particular contexts. For example, a bit sequence can be thought of—in some contexts—as an integer in binary notation; using that abstraction, it makes sense to divide the integer by 3 and get another sequence of bits that is the quotient. But in a context that abstracts bit sequences as images, it would not be reasonable to divide *Sunflowers* by 3 and get something meaningful, nor would it make sense to divide a DNA sequence by 3. But the abstraction of bits as, for example, images, should permit operations that make no sense on integers, such as cropping (removing bits that represent pixels at the edges of an image) or applying a watercolor filter in an image-manipulation program. Similarly, the abstraction of bits as DNA sequences should permit analysis of differences among plant species that would make no sense for integers or images.

Abstraction also makes it possible to perceive and manipulate the same computer-represented "object" at many levels. Objects at one level make available to higher levels a fixed set of operations, and are perceived by the higher level as if these were the only operations that could ever be performed on them. For example, the bit sequence representing *Sunflowers* and other paintings could be thought of as part of a *relation* (two-dimensional table of data), in which each row contains the bits representing an image, another bit sequence representing the name of the painting, a third bit sequence representing the name of the artist, and so on. At the lowest level, there are operations that manipulate the individual entries in each row; for example, the image bit string could be converted to a black and white image by manipulating the color information. At the next level, one considers the entire relation as an object; operations on the relation, rather than manipulating pixels or displaying images, instead perform such operations as "find all the images of paintings by

Van Gogh." If the image abstraction permitted operations like "tell if this image has a region that the typical person would perceive as a sunflower," then the relation abstraction would permit searches like "find the names of all paintings with one or more sunflowers in them." Alas, that sort of operation on images is beyond the state of the art at the beginning of the 21st century. However, operations at the image-level abstraction can be used to determine if an image has a large region of yellowish-orange, and thus to support a question at the level of the table such as "find the names of paintings with large yellow-orange regions."

As alluded to above, abstractions apply to procedures as well as data. Consider a bit sequence representing a piece of computer code that performs a sequence of operations on *Sunflowers*. One set of bits might provide the (detailed) machine instructions to display the image on a particular computer. Another set of bits might be the program to animate a model of a sunflower blowing in the breeze—when interpreted by the compiler for that language (and, of course, when the object code is then executed). Yet a third set of bits might be in an animation language that permits the motion of a sunflower to be described at a high level.

The print function common across applications on most systems today, which allows a wide range of data objects to be printed on a wide range of printers, is a powerful example of abstraction. The user need not know about all the details hiding behind this simple interface—the "print" command is an abstraction that shows the user only what he or she needs to see.

In each case, the bits are interpreted by a model that abstracts procedures above the actual machine instructions that a computer executes. Observe also that bits can at the same time be both data and procedure— the compiler reads a program to produce an output (data) that will later be executed by a computer (procedure).

The Internet works today because of abstractions that were products of the human imagination. Computer scientists imagined "packets" of information flowing through pipes, and they (symbolically) worked out the consequences of that idea to determine the new laws those flows of information must obey. This conceptualization led to the development of protocols that govern how data flows through the Internet, what happens when packets get lost, and so on. The Internet's constructs extend well beyond mathematics or models to high-level design principles such as keeping the network core simple and keeping detailed functionality at the edges. The power of a good abstraction is illustrated by the fact that the Internet's basic protocols have reliably carried traffic on the network since its creation, even as this traffic has changed enormously not just in scale but also in behavior, from e-mail to streaming media and peer-to-peer file sharing networks.

In Part Two, Shaw (in Chapter 4) presents abstractions as a key idea in software design. The essay by Aho and Larus (in Chapter 4) discusses how the abstractions in computer languages bridge the gap between computer hardware and humans. Programming languages offer ways to encapsulate the details of algorithms and define procedural and data abstractions that allow the algorithms to be used without knowledge of their details. Peterson and Clark (in Chapter 7) discuss the important abstractions of the Internet, and Gray (in Chapter 5) covers abstractions that have proved especially useful for representing data.

Computer Science Research Creates and Studies Algorithms

Often, computing research is less about how to represent static objects (such as an image or a driver's-license record) and more about developing and studying *algorithms* (precise ways to do a particular task) that will perform operations on objects. With respect to images, such operations might include cropping an image, finding boundaries between regions of different color or texture, or telling whether an image has at least 20 percent of its colors between yellow and orange. Given a symbolic representation of a sunflower as a set of measurements and some assumptions about the strength of the stem and the force of a breeze, a virtual reality algorithm could display that sunflower swaying in the breeze. Programming languages offer ways to encapsulate the details of these algorithms and define procedural abstractions that allow the algorithms to be used without requiring knowledge of their details.

Computer science also concerns itself with the amount of time an algorithm takes (its *running time*), and some computer scientists try to find algorithms that take less time than others to do similar things, sometimes dramatically reducing the time required. It would not do if, for example, it took all day to tell if a typical-sized image were 20 percent yellow. Sometimes, such research yields major breakthroughs that offer order-of-magnitude improvements in the time required to solve a particular type of problem.

Part Two includes a discussion of programming languages in Aho and Larus (in Chapter 4) and a treatment of algorithms and their running time in Kleinberg and Papadimitriou (in Chapter 2). Indeed, essentially all the essays in this volume mention algorithms and/or programming-language representations for one or another kind of information.

Computer Science Research Creates Artificial Constructs, Notably Unlimited by Physical Laws

Animated sunflowers blowing in the breeze are an example of how the computational world can mimic, at an extremely accurate level, the behavior of the real world. While computer scientists often addresses the world as it is, computer science also deals with the world as it could be, or with an entirely invented world behaving under different assumptions. Computer scientists can, for example, easily change the rules, making water more viscous or weakening the effect of gravity. For example, video-game characters often obey physical laws that have never been seen in nature ("Roadrunner physics"). Computational models also describe complex natural phenomena that are hard to observe in nature. Such models can describe both natural and unnatural worlds. For example, it is entirely possible to make ocean waves a bit more exciting to watch by altering gravity or the viscosity of water—changes impossible in the laboratory but routine within the world of computing.

Fedkiw (in Chapter 3) describes how computer-generated animation produces such images as the waves in the movie *The Perfect Storm*. Peterson and Clark (in Chapter 7) describe the Internet model. Bruckman (in Chapter 7) examines online virtual communities.

Computer Science Research Exploits and Addresses Exponential Growth

The speed of light doesn't change at all, and DNA strands have grown in length only over geologic time. But computer science must deal with machines that, by various measures of size and speed (for fixed cost), double in performance roughly every $1^1/_2$ to 2 years (see the essay on Moore's law by Hill in Chapter 2).[2] Although these performance improvements make it easier for computer scientists to solve some problems, they can also magnify computer and system design challenges. Over time, the critical resource to be optimized changes; designers today must take into account that obtaining two numbers from a computer's main memory can take a hundred times longer than multiplying them together whereas just the opposite was once true. Moreover, the improvements create commensurate demands that the machines be used to solve ever more complex problems and larger or harder instances of the same problem and that ever-larger systems be built.

---

[2]There are really two related trends that go by the name Moore's law. The original form of Moore's law states that the number of transistors per chip doubles every 18 months. The popular form of Moore's law states that as a result of increasing transistor density and other technological progress, such as the density of magnetic disk drives, the performance of a comparable-cost computer doubles roughly every $1^1/_2$ to 2 years or, alternatively, that the cost for the same performance halves. This combination of extremely rapid exponential growth and the ability to exploit the improvements in many different combinations of cost and performance is unprecedented in the history of technology.

Computer scientists have a rule of thumb that every time things get 10 times larger or faster a qualitatively different class of research challenges emerges. To get a sense of this, suppose you are playing bridge, and you need to examine your hand to see whether you hold no cards of the suit being played, and therefore are allowed to trump the trick. Since your hand consists of at most 13 cards at any time, you can usually figure it out quickly by scanning each of your cards. But suppose bridge were played with hands of a million cards, with 10,000 suits, each of 100 ranks. Could you figure out which card to play before your opponents got up to get a snack? Computers deal with similar situations all the time, and to avoid scanning all 1,000,000 cards, organizations for data have been devised that allow us to design algorithms that home in on the desired card much more quickly than can the obvious "scan all cards" algorithm.

The expectation of rapid improvement in capabilities leads to a form of research, perhaps unique to computer science, sometimes called "living in the future." Although almost every technology goes through some period of exponential growth, computers are remarkable because the doubling time is unusually short and the exponential growth period has been unusually long. As a result, it often makes sense to think about what the world will be like when computing machines are 10 times faster, or able to communicate with 100 times the bandwidth. Certain things that one cannot now do, or cannot do for a reasonable cost, are suddenly going to become possible. Many research successes that turned into successful products were the result of such confident, forward thinking.

In addition to Hill's, many of the essays in this volume show how computer science research has both exploited the exponential improvement in our tools and dealt with the exponential growth in requirements. The essay by Koller and Biermann (in Chapter 6) examines chess playing, where the goals of being able to defeat better and better players have largely been met. Peterson and Clark (in Chapter 7) show how we are coping with the ever-growing Internet.

Computer Science Research Seeks the Fundamental Limits on What Can Be Computed

In addition to developing knowledge that supports practical engineering applications, computer science investigates fundamental limits regarding computation. It has been known since the 1930s that there are *undecidable* problems, those that can be stated succinctly yet cannot be answered. The canonical example of these is, can you write a computer program that given an arbitrary program P and arbitrary input N to that program, can answer the question, does the program P ever stop running when given the input N? The discovery that the answer to this question is no is fundamental in the sense that it applies to all possible programs rather than being a statement about a particular piece of programming code.

Perhaps more important is the discovery that not everything that is decidable (a computer can solve it, somehow) is *tractable* (solvable in sufficiently little time that we can expect to get answers to reasonably large instances of the problem in reasonable time). Some problems, such as searching for cards described above, are tractable. Even the dumb algorithm of examining each one of n cards in one's hand would only take time proportional to n. However, there are other problems that are not tractable—where time or computing resources proportional to the size of the instance to be solved are insufficient. Instead, they require time or resources that are exponential in the size of the input n—that is, time that grows like 2^n. This sort of analysis extends more generally to how the required computing resources relate to the nature and structure of a problem as well as its size. For some types of problems, the issue is how accurately something can be computed; here computer science seeks an understanding of the fundamental limits in the accuracy of what can be computed and the accuracy of what can be computed quickly (as in approximation algorithms).

An example of a tractability problem is the Traveling Salesman Problem (TSP), where one is given n "cities" (nodes of a graph) with distances between each pair. The goal is for the salesman (who, following our earlier example, is selling sunflower oil) to visit each city once and return to the starting city, but minimize the total distance traveled. An obvious solution, starting from one of the n cities, has $n - 1$ choices for the first city, $n - 2$ choices for the next, and so on, a total of $(n - 1)(n - 2) \ldots (2)(1)$ choices. Unfortunately, this number of choices grows faster than 2^n. What is worse, the theory of intractable problems provides powerful evidence that there is no way to solve the TSP in substantially less time. As a result, even the exponential improvement in the speed of computers ("Moore's law," as mentioned above) can do almost nothing to increase the size of problem instance that can be dealt with; perhaps one can handle a few more cities each year, at best. Of course, even when it is impractical to solve a problem generally and optimally, the situation is not necessarily hopeless. In practice, salesmen can make their rounds fairly efficiently because algorithms that do well enough most of the time have been discovered.

The fundamental limit on our ability to compute applies not only to the TSP, but also to thousands of problems encountered daily. That is, one can solve these problems by computer only when the problem instance is rather small, and the situation can never get much better. Research on fundamental limits thus informs practical application, by showing that some system designs are ultimately a dead end.

In Part Two, Kleinberg and Papadimitriou (in Chapter 2) provide a discussion of the precise implications of the theory of intractable problems, and Sudan (in Chapter 7) discusses cryptography, a domain where the intractability of a problem is a help, not a hindrance, because the goal is assurance that an intruder with a fast computer cannot discover secrets within any reasonable amount of time.

Computer Science Research Often Focuses on the Complex, Analytic, Rational Action That Is Associated with Human Intelligence

One aspiration of computer science has been to understand and emulate capabilities that are associated with intelligent human behavior. One class of these activities is devoted to enabling computers to solve problems that humans can solve easily, yet that appear very difficult for machines. A human can easily pick out the presence of a sunflower in an image, and yet a computer of the early 21st century can do so only with difficulty and limited accuracy. The problems of image understanding, language understanding, locomotion, game playing, and problem solving each provide enormous challenges for the computer scientist. A second class of intelligence-related research is to understand how the human mind works by trying to solve problems the way humans do. It turns out, for example, that the simple "if A then B" logic harking back to Aristotle does not capture nearly enough of the way people think and make inferences about their environment. A third class of intelligence-related research is enabling computers to interact with the world by enabling them to sense the environment, move within it, and manipulate objects.

These efforts are elaborated in several of the essays. In Chapter 6, Koller and Biermann discuss game playing by computer as a testbed for approaches that emulate intelligence. Lee tells about approaches to computer understanding of natural language. Mitchell explores the development of machine-learning techniques.

Part Two of this volume explores some of the depth and breadth of computer science through essays written by computer scientists. The essays provide several researchers' own views about their research areas and convey what excites these researchers about computer science.

Part Two

Selected Perspectives on Computer Science

The character of computer science research can perhaps best be appreciated by seeing some of the things computer scientists do and why they choose to do them. In Part Two, computer scientists explain not only some of the results achieved in several areas of computer science research but also what interests and excites them about the research. The diversity of the topics addressed in these essays reflects the diversity of the field itself.

The essays in Part Two are organized by chapter into several clusters:

- *Exponential growth, computability, and complexity.* How computer science research makes possible a sustained growth in computing power and how theoretical models of computation help us understand intrinsic limits on what is computable (Chapter 2).
- *Simulation.* How computer models can be used to simulate aspects of the physical world (Chapter 3).
- *Abstraction, representation, and notations.* How abstraction is used to express understanding of a problem, manage complexity, and select the appropriate level of detail and degree of generality (Chapter 4).
- *Data, representation, and information.* How computer science has developed new ways of storing, retrieving, and manipulating data, and how these techniques can profoundly influence the models of a wide range of professionals (Chapter 5).
- *Achieving intelligence.* How computer science's aspiration to emulate human intelligence has resulted in advances in machine learning,

computers' natural-language understanding, and improved strategies for game-like situations (Chapter 6).

 • *Building computing systems of practical scale.* How the design, development, and large-scale deployment of working computing systems—notably, the Internet—not only are of great practical value but also constitute a diverse and fruitful area of research by which computer scientists may improve these systems and create new ones (Chapter 7).

 • *Research behind everyday computation.* How computer scientists' efforts in the service of human effectiveness have led to such advances as spreadsheets, text-formatting programs, and information retrieval from the Internet, and how these and other innovations have had a very broad impact (Chapter 8).

 • *Personal passion about computer science research.* How several computer scientists explain their commitment to computer science research (Chapter 9).

2

Exponential Growth, Computability, and Complexity

The essay by Hill that follows describes how exponential growth in computing capability drives technological and intellectual progress and how computer science research works to sustain this remarkable growth.

Next, Kleinberg and Papadimitriou address the intellectual essence of computation. They provide glimpses not only into the foundational models that define computation but also into theoreticians' thinking about these models—what's convincing, what's surprising, what's not.

Finally, Bennett describes how quantum computing research seeks to dodge a fundamental physical limit of current computing technology and stretch our conception of computation.

HARNESSING MOORE'S LAW

Mark D. Hill, University of Wisconsin, Madison

For most products, the claim "better and cheaper" casts suspicion on the salesperson. For computer-related products, however, "better and cheaper" has been wildly true for decades. In this essay, we seek to explain this success so as to give readers a foundation with which to appreciate what the future might hold. Specifically, we explain how rapid technological progress (e.g., the technologist's Moore's law) has been harnessed to enable better and cheaper computers (the popular media's Moore's law). We then touch upon future prospects for technological progress, computer implementation challenges, and potential impacts.

How Does Computer Hardware Work?

Before delving into our rapid progress in improving computers, it is important to reflect on how computers work. As discussed in Chapter 1 of this volume, computers are not designed to perform a single task. Instead they are machines that can perform many different computational tasks, including tasks that are not specified or even conceived until after the computer is deployed.

We enable this flexibility by using *software*. Software represents a computational task to hardware as a collection of commands. Each command is called an *instruction* and the set of instructions that the hardware supports—its vocabulary—is its *instruction set architecture*. Most instructions are simple. An "add" instruction adds two numbers and indicates which instruction is next. A "branch" instruction compares two numbers to choose which instruction is next. The instructions manipulate *data*, such as numbers and characters.

Moreover, instructions can manipulate other instructions, since most modern computers store instructions just like data. Treating instructions as data enables programs, such as *compilers*, that can translate high-level language programs (e.g., written in Java) into machine instructions (see Aho and Larus in Chapter 4).

Computer hardware has three basic components:

• A *processor* executes instructions. Today, it is most common to implement a processor on a single silicon chip called a *microprocessor*. Most computers today employ a single microprocessor, but larger computers employ multiple microprocessors.

• *Memory* stores instructions and data. Current desktop computer memories are implemented in several chips and backed up by one or more magnetic disks. Larger computers can employ hundreds of memory chips and disks.

• *Input/output* devices connect a computer to both humans (e.g., keyboards, displays, mice, and speakers) (see Foley in Chapter 8) and to other computers via networks (see Peterson and Clark in Chapter 7).

Hardware designers seek to make processors that execute instructions faster, memory that provides more information, and input/output devices that communicate more effectively. Furthermore, we can and do focus on making these primitive elements faster without worrying about what the software running on the hardware is actually doing.

But how do we know this all works? Why is relatively simple hardware sufficient for most computing? Which instructions do I need in my instruction set architecture? Kleinberg and Papadimitriou in this chapter address these questions using the formal foundations of the Universal Turing Machine and the Church-Turing hypothesis. These foundations allow hardware designers to concentrate on the practical questions of engineering effective hardware.

Moore's Law and Exponential Growth

The key enabler of "better and cheaper" computers has been rapid technological progress. Arguably, the most important enabler has been the progress in the number of transistors (switches) per semiconductor integrated circuit (chip). In 1965, Gordon Moore used four data points to predict that the number of transistors per chip would double every 2 years. He was not far off! The trend over the last 35 years has indeed been exponential, with the number of transistors per chip doubling approximately every 18 months. Technologists call this trend *Moore's law*.

Some commentators have implied that exponential growth, such as with Moore's law, is unique to computer technology. This belief is incorrect. In fact, exponential growth is common and occurs whenever the rate of increase of a quantity is proportional to the size of the quantity. Examples include compound interest and unconstrained biological population growth. For example, $100 earning compound interest at a rate of 10 percent will more than double in 8 years: $214 = $100 \times (1 + 0.10)^8$.

To understand the implications of rapid exponential growth, consider the absurd example of your annual salary starting at a modest $16 but then doubling every 18 months for 36 years. This improvement corresponds to an annual growth rate of 59 percent. In the early years, your finances would be very tight (e.g., $64 after 3 years). You would have to live with your parents. With patience, you will eventually be able to buy a car ($16,000 after 15 years). Then you can move out and buy a house

($100,000 after 24 years). Eventually you will be very rich and have to dream up fundamentally new ways to spend money ($300 million after 36 years).

The potency of Moore's law is evident when we observe that it has followed the rate and duration of the absurd income example just given. Sixteen transistors per chip is a mid-1960s number, while 300 million transistors per chip is an early 21st century count. Of course, Moore's law is not a law of nature. Rather it is a business expectation in the semiconductor industry: to stay even with their competitors, technologists should solve the problems to double the number of transistors per chip every 18 months.

Fortunately, the number of transistors per chip is not the only technological aspect that is achieving rapid, exponential growth rates. The smaller transistors enabling Moore's law also switch much faster. Moreover, improvements rivaling (or exceeding) Moore's law have occurred in magnetic disk storage capacity and effective fiber optic network bandwidth.

Unfortunately, some other technologies are improving much more slowly, notably the round-trip delays to memory chips, to disks, and across networks. Memory chip delays are improving slowly because memory chip manufacturers optimize for larger memory capacity instead. Disk delays seem limited by the inertia of mechanically moving macroscopic mass, while network delays are ultimately limited by the speed of light.

How We Have Harnessed Exponential Growth

While it is obvious that rapid technological improvements provide great opportunities for implementing computers, it is also the case that rapid and differential rates pose great challenges. Rapid change means that ideas that were too wasteful (e.g., in number of transistors) soon become appropriate and then become inadequate. The processors in 1960s computers required hundreds or thousands of chips. It was not until 1970 that is was even possible to implement a primitive processor on a single chip (and that first so-called *microprocessor* could only access a memory of 300 bytes, i.e., 0.0003 megabytes!).

Subsequently, Moore's law enabled microprocessors to use more and faster transistors. New microprocessor designers exploited this transistor bonanza to obtain computers that got faster more rapidly than the transistors got faster. Central to this effort are methods of using many transistors to cooperate side-by-side in what we call *parallelism*. Not surprisingly, approaches for exploiting transistor parallelism depend on scale or "level" (much as approaches for organizing humans to work in parallel depend greatly on whether 10, 1000, or 1 million people are available). With transistors in a microprocessor, we have organized our focus on *bit* and *instruction* level parallelism. Near the end of this essay, we discuss how the currently modest use of *thread* level parallelism needs to be greatly expanded.

During the 1970s and earlier 1980s, microprocessor development focused on accelerating the execution of each instruction using *bit level parallelism*. Designers made changes to enable each instruction to both (a) manipulate a larger range of numbers (and symbols) and (b) perform those manipulations faster using more transistors side by side. Early microprocessors, for example, slowly performed manipulations on integers taking on one of 65,536 (2^{16}) values (or fewer). In a single instruction, a current microprocessor can rapidly transform data whose values range through billions (2^{32}) or quintillions (2^{64}) of integer and fractional values.

Since the mid-1980s, many microprocessor improvements have focused on parallelism between instructions, not within instructions, with what is called *instruction level parallelism*. Thus, instead of executing instruction A, then instruction B, and then instruction C, we try to do instructions A, B, and C at the same time. To exploit instruction level parallelism past a few instructions, however, it is necessary to predict the outcomes of program decisions (often embodied in branch instructions) and speculatively execute subsequent instructions. Instruction level parallelism techniques have been so successful that modern microprocessors can have several dozen instructions in execution at any one time! Nevertheless, most microprocessors still *appear* to execute instructions one at a time. This illusion allows these microprocessors to run existing software, unmodified. It enables performance gains without endangering the billions of dollars invested to develop and deploy existing software.

The fact that technologies progress at different rates also poses challenges to computer implementations. Twenty years ago, the time to execute a multiply instruction and the time to access a computer's main memory were comparable. Differential rates of improvement now make a multiplication more than 100 times faster than accessing main memory. Computer architects have responded with a plethora of types and layers of *caches*. Caches are smaller, faster memories that transparently hold the most-recently accessed subset of the information from a larger, slower memory. Caches are faster than main memory, because they are smaller (fewer bits to reach and select among) and can be implemented in technologies more optimized for speed. Caches often hold a very small fraction of the larger memory (e.g., a 64 kilobyte cache for a 64 megabyte memory). Nevertheless, they are able to satisfy a substantial fraction of requests quickly (e.g., 98 percent) due to *locality* (the property that, at many sizes and time scales, recently accessed information is highly likely to be re-accessed quickly). In some ways, caches work for reasons similar to why your cellular phone can hold many of the numbers you actually call. In fact, caches are so effective that current microprocessor designers spend most of their transistors on caches! More generally, caching benefits many aspects of computer systems, as locality is common and smaller memories are faster than larger ones in many technologies.

Meeting the above challenges has enabled computers whose performance has been doubling every 2 years. Ambiguously, this trend is also called *Moore's law* (e.g., by the popular press). At this point, we have two Moore's laws:

- *Technologist's Moore's law*: number of transistors per chip doubles every 18 months, and
- *Popular Moore's law:* computer performance doubles every 2 years.

This popular Moore's law has provided incredible opportunities for the rest of computer science. Everyone from researchers to product designers can dream up many ideas and ask not whether something will be practical, but *when* (assuming, of course, one is not trying to solve problems that cannot be solved or require execution times that defeat exponential growth with exponential complexity—see Kleinberg and Papadimitriou). This performance has facilitated major achievements, such as beating a chess grandmaster (Koller and Biermann, in Chapter 6), more realistic computer graphics (Fedkiw, in Chapter 3), better natural-language processing (Lee, in Chapter 6), and sequencing the human genome. In these and other cases, however, tremendous algorithmic and software advances were also necessary to effectively use faster hardware.

Many times, however, cost reduction matters more than increasing performance. In these cases, rather than using more transistors to obtain more performance at constant cost, it makes more sense to use a constant number of transistors to obtain the same performance at reduced cost. Fortuitously, it turns out that every 2 years or so one can obtain *the same level of performance for half the cost*. In a decade, Jim Gray has observed, it will be possible to buy an equivalent computer for the sales tax on one today (even if the sales tax is as low as 3 percent, which approximately equals $1/2^5$). Cost matters because more cost-effective computation can effectively be more widely applied. This cost reduction has enabled the rapid spread of inexpensive computers and enabled the explosive growth of the Internet (Peterson and Clark, in Chapter 7). Once again, creative innovations, such as word processors (Ullman, in Chapter 8), spreadsheets (Foley, in Chapter 8), and compelling multi-user environments (Bruckman, in Chapter 7) are necessary to make cost-effective hardware useful.

Future of Moore's Law and Beyond

Recently, there have been several accounts predicting the end of the technologist's Moore's law. Since at least the early 1970s, there have been numerous predictions of its demise. However, technologists' creativity has repeatedly solved the challenges to keep it on track. We are bullish that Moore's law is safe for at least another decade, due to technologies already operating in the laboratory, backed by the motivation and vision of a trillion-dollar industry.[1]

Nevertheless, it seems probable that the doubling time for conventional chips will increase and the doubling will eventually halt as atomic limits are approached. There is already evidence that the doubling time for memory chips is now closer to every 2 years instead of every 18 months. A contributing factor to this slowdown is the exponentially increasing cost of building factories for fabricating chips.

Taking a longer view, however, innovation beyond the technologist's Moore's law is likely. Computing has already been implemented by a series of technologies: mechanical switches, vacuum tubes, discrete transistors, and now chips driven by Moore's law. Eventually, almost all computing technologies will be supplanted by newer ones. One emerging candidate uses synthetic organic molecules to perform switching and storage. Another seeks to exploit quantum superposition to change both the model and the implementation of some future computers (see Bennett in this chapter). Both approaches, however, are unproven and may yet be surpassed by other technologies, some of which are not yet invented.

Moreover, we are not yet close to "fundamental" limits. We are many orders of magnitude from subatomic energy and storage limits imposed by currently understood physics. Furthermore, there is an existence proof that it is possible to organize computers in a way that is much better for many tasks: the human brain.

As an aside, some argue that we do not need more computing performance. While it is indeed the case that other constraints, such as low power, low noise, and low environmental impact, are becoming more important, we argue for more cost-effective computer performance. First, all past predictions that there was enough computing performance have been wrong. Two decades ago, some predicted that the ultimate personal computer would support three M's: one million instructions per second, one megabyte, and one million display elements. Today's personal computers routinely exceed the first two attributes by two orders of magnitude and still seem inadequate. Second, there are clear opportunities of

---

[1]See the International Technology Roadmap for Semiconductors Web site at http://public.itrs.net.

applying more computing performance (and more algorithms) to make human-computer interactions closer to the natural-language exchanges envisioned in *2001: A Space Odyssey* a third of a century ago. Third, as computing and communication get more cost-effective, surprising new applications are likely to be invented. Some of us used mainframes for decades without predicting the spreadsheet, while others used the Internet for years without predicting the World Wide Web. It will be surprising if an order-of-magnitude improvement in cost-effective computer performance does not enable a new disruptive application.

Harnessing Future Exponential Growth

In the coming decades, we seek to harness future technology growth, be it slow, fast, or discontinuous. How will we use more transistors (or more exotic technologies) to enable hardware that will support the creative applications being forecast in the rest of this volume?

How do we exploit billions and trillions of transistors? (A computer with one gigabyte of memory, for example, has more than 8 billion transistors.) One known way is to go beyond bit- and instruction-level parallelism to also exploit *thread-level* parallelism. When a processor executes a sequence of instructions, we say it is executing a thread. Thread-level parallelism is exploited when software specifies multiple threads to execute and hardware is capable of executing the threads concurrently. Today, several important applications are specified with multiple threads, including database management systems (Gray, in Chapter 5) and Web crawlers (Norvig, in Chapter 8); multiple threading is also used to beat human chess champions (Koller and Biermann, in Chapter 6). Unfortunately, too many current applications are programmed with a single thread, even if the problem could be solved in parallel. Much established business software, for example, was written for a single thread, even when the problem was once solved by many clerks operating in parallel. Nevertheless, creating multi-threaded software has been difficult. In addition, the motivation to create it has been reduced by the fact that many current computers execute only one thread at a time. Emerging techniques for supporting multiple threads on a microprocessor, however, promise to make multi-threading hardware much more widely available. Moreover, there is also tremendous additional potential for using threads executing in parallel on multiple computers that communicate via local- or wide-area networks. In the extreme, computers around the world could be harnessed to solve problems on demand. This vision is now known as grid computing, since it strives to deliver customers access to computing resources much as the power grid delivers customers power. We encourage future efforts to exploit parallel threads in all their forms, because doing so represents the best-known way to grow computing performance much faster than Moore's law enables for single processors.

We also see additional opportunity provided by technology discontinuities and synergies. First, Moore's law will soon enable a complete (albeit simple) computer on a chip. Today's personal computers, for example, use a complete processor on a chip—the microprocessor—together with several memory and support chips. Single-chip computers could dramatically cut costs and expand the effectiveness of systems. While we have primitive single-chip systems today, more powerful ones might unleash progress in a manner similar to that unleashed by the increasing performance of microprocessors over the last three decades. For at least the next decade, however, single-chip solutions must focus on systems smaller than personal computers (because personal computers use too much memory to fit on a chip). Nevertheless, the history of computing has shown that new smaller systems are great catalysts for change: mainframes to minicomputers to personal computers to personal digital assistants to cellular phones. Second, technologists are now fabricating sensors and emitters on chips. This technology holds the promise of systems that integrate with their environment at unprecedently low cost. A current success story is an accelerometer for triggering automobile airbag deployment. Third, the further integration of computers with communication will make the world even smaller. Communication, with and without wires, will enable ubiquitous connectivity. The World Wide Web shows us how communication magnifies the value of computation. Now, imagine a Web where you are always online everywhere!

Each of these trends will further integrate computers into our lives. In many cases, integration allows the computers to "disappear." When Emily clicked to buy a book in the prelude to this volume, she was not even aware of most of the computers that implemented the transaction. Furthermore, she may not recognize her cellular phone, personal digital assistant, or pacemaker as computers; an integration that is an appropriate and natural consequence of our abilities to hide complexity from users.

Our success in hiding computers when they work, however, brings with it a responsibility to hide them when they fail. Imagine Web services as available as telephones and personal computers as dependable as televisions. Numerous solutions will be needed to enable this dependability, taking into account needs and appropriate costs. Large commercial systems may seek 10 to 100 times improvements in availability for small overheads (e.g., 10 percent), while critical functions like pacemakers may tolerate tripling hardware costs. In many cases, the underlying hardware may get more unreliable, because transistors are so small (and susceptible to cosmic rays) and numerous (more chances to fail). While some improvements can be done in hardware, transparently to software, other solutions will require hardware and software changes. In many cases, we will have to design systems assuming that parts will fail. Unlike the current Web, however, we should seek to ensure that all systems mask almost all of those failures from users. By laying a more reliable foundation, we can expand the realms in which society can depend on information technology.

The last half-century has seen substantial computing advances and impacts on society. We expect the synergies just discussed to provide plenty of non-technical and technical challenges and opportunities. For society, the real information revolution may be coming soon. On the technical side, there is much work to be done. Arthur C. Clarke said, "Any sufficiently advanced technology is indistinguishable from magic." Let's create some more magic!

COMPUTABILITY AND COMPLEXITY

Jon Kleinberg, Cornell University, and
Christos Papadimitriou, University of California, Berkeley

The Quest for the Quintic Formula

One of the great obsessions of Renaissance sages was the solution of polynomial equations: find an x that causes a certain polynomial to evaluate to 0. Today we all learn in school how to solve quadratic equations (polynomial equations of degree two, such as $ax^2 + bx + c = 0$), even though many of us have to look up the formula every time (it's $x = 1/2a\left(-b \pm \sqrt{b^2 - 4ac}\right)$). Versions of this formula were known to the Babylonians as early as 2000 BC, and they were rediscovered in many ancient cultures. The discovery of similar but much more complicated formulas for solving equations of degree three and four—the cubic and quartic formulae—had to wait until the 16th century AD. During the next three centuries, the greatest minds in Europe strove unsuccessfully to discover the quintic formula, cracking equations of degree five, until the flowering of modern algebra brought the quest to a sudden, surprising resolution: a proof that *there is no quintic formula*.

This story, on first hearing, can engender a few natural reactions. Among them, surprise—what's the obstacle to a quintic formula? Why was it so hard to prove it didn't exist? And, more subtly, a mild sense of perplexity—what do we mean by a quintic formula anyway? Why can't we write "the largest x such that $ax^5 + bx^4 + cx^3 + dx^2 + ex + f = 0$" and declare this to be a formula?

So we back up. By a "formula" in this story, we meant a particular thing: a finite sequence of steps that begins with the given values of the coefficients and ends with a root x; each step consists of one of the basic arithmetic operations applied to certain of the quantities already computed, or else it consists of the extraction of a root of one of the quantities already computed. Now we can assert more precisely, thanks to the work of the 19th-century mathematicians Abel and Galois: there is no quintic formula.

Viewed from the safe distance of a few centuries, the story is clearly one about computation, and it contains many of the key ingredients that arise in later efforts to model computation: We take a computational process that we understand intuitively (solving an equation, in this case), formulate a precise model, and from the model derive some highly unexpected consequences about the computational power of the process. It is precisely this approach that we wish to apply to computation in general. But moving from this example to a fully general model of computation requires some further fundamental ideas, because the notion of a "formula"—a straight-line recipe of arithmetic operations—omits two of the crucial properties of general-purpose computation. First, computation can be repetitive; we should be able to perform some action over and over until a certain stopping condition is satisfied. Second, computation should contain "adaptive" steps of the following form: test whether a certain condition is satisfied; if it is, then perform action A; if it isn't, then perform action B. Neither of these is present in straight-line formulas; but a little reflection convinces one that they are necessary to specify many of the other activities that we would consider computational.

Computation as a Universal Technology

So, guided by this intuition, let us move beyond stylized forms of computation and seek to understand general-purpose computation in all its richness—for if we could do this, then we might find similarly surprising consequences that apply much more broadly. Such was the goal of Alan Turing in the 1930s, and such was also the goal of a host of other mathematical logicians at that time.

Turing's entry in this field is particularly compelling, not so much because of its mathematical elegance but because of its basic, common-sensical motivation and power. He sought a streamlined mathematical description of what goes on when a person is performing calculations in a large notebook: he or she writes down and erases symbols, turns the pages left or right, keeps a limited number of symbols in his or her memory. The computing device Turing proposed—the Turing machine—has access to an infinite sequence of "pages," each of which can hold only one symbol. At any time, the machine can be in one of a finite set of possible "states of mind"—its working memory. The flow of control proceeds simply as follows: based on its current state, and the symbol it is currently reading, the machine may write a new symbol on the current page (erasing the existing one), move to the next or preceding page, and change its state. Subject to these rules, the Turing machine processes the input it is given and may eventually choose to halt, at which point the notebook contains its output.

Why should we accept this model? First, it accords well with common sense. It seems to be the way that symbolic computation, as performed slowly and painfully by humans, proceeds. Indeed, with some practice, one can implement seemingly any natural symbolic task on a Turing machine. Second, it is robust—a version of the model with very small sets of available symbols and states (say, eight of each) is, in a precise sense, just as powerful as a version with an arbitrary finite set of each, only the control rules become more complicated. Moreover, it does not matter that the "pages" on which the computation is performed are arranged in a linear sequence; it would not add to the power of the model if we arranged them instead in an arbitrary web of connections. Finally, and most crucially, Turing's model is precisely equivalent to the other formalisms proposed in his day, among them, and preceding it, Alonzo Church's lambda calculus—and it is also equivalent to modern general-purpose programming languages such as C and Java (with access to an arbitrary amount of memory).

For the accumulation of these reasons, we are justified in believing that we have arrived at the "right" model of computation; and this is the content of the Church-Turing thesis: a symbolic function is computable if and only if it can be computed on a Turing machine (or its equivalents). It is important to notice what is being claimed: we have not derived the notion of "computability" from a set of more primitive axioms; rather, after extensive thought experiments, we have asserted that "computability" corresponds precisely to what can be computed on a Turing machine.

Accepting the Turing machine as the basis for our precise definition of computability is a momentous step. Its first consequence is that of universality: there is a "universal Turing machine" U that does the following. As input, U receives the description of a Turing machine M (the "code" of M, written in U's book) and an input n to M (a later chapter in the same book). As output, U returns the result, if any, of running M on n. Today, we would think of U simply as an interpreter—it executes a step-by-step simulation of any Turing machine M presented to it. Indeed, our style of writing programs and then executing them is so ingrained in our view of computation that it takes a moment to appreciate the consequences that flow from a universal machine. It means that programs and data are really the same thing: a program is just a sequence of symbols that looks like any other piece of input; but when fed to a universal machine, this input wakes up and begins to compute. Think of mobile code, Java applets, e-mail viruses: your computer downloads them as data and then runs them as programs.

The principle of interchangeable parts—that components of a machine can be mass-produced independently, and a working whole can be assembled from a random selection of one part from each kind—was the disruptive insight that underpinned the Industrial Revolution. Universality is perhaps an even more radical approach to assembling systems: a single computer on your desk can run your word processor, your spreadsheet, and your online calendar, as well as new applications not yet conceived of or written. And while this may seem completely natural, most of technology in fact does not work this way at all. In most aspects of one's technological life, the device is the application; they are one and the same. If you own a radio and want to watch TV, you must buy a new device. If you want to drive, you use a car; but if you want to fly, you use an airplane. Your car cannot download a new set of instructions and suddenly be able to fly, or to maneuver underwater. But the computational world has a flexibility of application that cannot really be imagined elsewhere—and that is because the world of computation is powered by universal machines.

We have all seen the consequences of this flexibility very clearly in the past decade, as the World Wide Web became a new medium within a mere 7 years of its introduction. If we look at other media—at the phone, the radio, the television—it took a much longer time from their inceptions to widespread prominence. What was the difference? Of course there are many factors that one can point to, but mingled among them is the universality of the computers on which Web protocols and interfaces run. People had already bought personal computers for their homes, and built office information systems around them, before the Web ever existed. When the Web arrived, it could spread through this infrastructure with amazing speed. One cannot really imagine an analogue of this process for the television—it would be as though millions of Americans had been induced to buy large inert boxes for their living rooms, and a decade later someone dreamed up the technology to begin broadcasting pictures to them. But this is more or less what happened with the Web.

The Limits of Computation

Computer science was born knowing its own limitations. For the strength of the universal machine leads directly to a second, and more negative, consequence—uncomputability, the fact that certain natural computational tasks cannot be carried out by Turing machines or, by extension, computer programs. The leap from the notion of universality to this impossibility result is surprisingly effortless, if ingenious. It is rooted in two basic issues—first, the surprising difficulty in determining the "ultimate" behavior of a program; and second, the self-referential character of the universal machine U.

To appreciate the first of these, recall that our universal machine U simply performed a step-by-step simulation of a Turing machine M on an input n. This means that if M computes forever, never halting, then U's simulation of M will run forever as well. This is the notion of an "infinite loop," familiar to beginning (and experienced) programmers everywhere—your program keeps running with no sign of any output. Do you stop it and see what's wrong, or wait to see if it's just taking longer than expected to come up with an answer? We might well want something stronger than the blind simulation that U provides; we might want a "Universal Termination Detector"—a Turing machine D that behaves as follows. Given a description of a Turing machine M and an input n to M, the machine D performs a finite number of steps, and then correctly reports whether or not M will ever halt with a result when it is run on n. (So in particular, the machine D itself halts on every input.)

Could one build such a thing? One's first reaction is to start dreaming up tricks by which one could look at a program and determine whether it will halt or not—looking for obviously repetitive behavior with no stopping condition. But gradually the problem begins to look hopelessly difficult. Maybe the program you're analyzing for termination is systematically enumerating the natural numbers, searching for a counter-example to a famous conjecture in mathematics; and it will only stop when it finds one. So a demonstration that this single program eventually terminates must implicitly resolve this mathematical conjecture! Could detecting the termination of programs really be as hard as automating mathematics?

This thought experiment raises the suggestion that we should perhaps be considering the problem from the other direction, trying to show that it is not possible to build a Universal Termination Detector. Another line of reasoning that might make us start considering such an impossibility result is, as suggested above, the self-referential nature of the universal machine U: U is a Turing machine that can simulate the behavior of any Turing machine. So, in particular, we could run U on a description of itself; what would happen? When you find yourself asking questions like this about a mathematical object—questions in which the object refers to itself—there are often explosive consequences lying just ahead. Indeed, the dangerous properties of self-reference appear in ordinary discourse. From ancient Greece we have Eubulides' paradox, which asserts, "This statement is false": is this a true statement or a false one? Or consider Bertrand Russell's hypothetical barber, who only shaves the set of all people who do not shave themselves—who then shaves the barber himself?

In the case at hand, we can exploit the self-reference inherent in universality to prove that there is no Universal Termination Detector by showing that there is no Turing machine that correctly implements a Universal Termination Detector (Box 2.1).

This is a first, fundamental impossibility result for computation—a natural problem that cannot be solved computationally. And starting with this result, impossibility spreads like a shock wave through the space of problems. We might want a Universal Equivalence Tester: given two Turing machines M and M', are they equivalent? Do they produce the same result on every input? But it is easy to convince yourself that if we could build an Equivalence Tester, we could use it to build a Termination Detector, which we know cannot exist. And so: There is no Universal Equivalence Tester. We might want a Universal Code Verifier: given a

BOX 2.1
There Is No Universal Termination Detector

We begin by observing that the set of all Turing machines, while clearly infinite, can be enumerated in a list *M1; M2; M3*, . . . in such a way that each Turing machine appears once in the list.

To do this, we can write a description of each Turing machine as a sequence of symbols and then order these descriptions in alphabetical order; we first list all descriptions with one symbol (if there are any), then all descriptions with two symbols, and so forth.

Our impossibility proof proceeds by assuming that there exists a Universal Termination Detector; we then show how this leads to a contradiction, establishing that our initial assumption cannot be valid. So to begin, let *D* be a Turing machine that is a Universal Termination Detector.

We construct, from *D*, a Turing machine *X* that will lead to the contradiction. On input *n*, here is what *X* does. It first invokes the Termination Detector *D* to determine whether the machine M_n will ever halt when run with input *n*. (This is the core of the self-reference: we investigate the behavior of M_n on its own position *n* in the alphabetical listing of Turing machines.) If it turns out that M_n will never halt on *n*, then *X* halts. But if it turns out that M_n will halt when run on *n*, then *X* gratuitously throws itself into an infinite loop, never halting.

X is not a very useful program; but that is not the point. The point is to notice that *X* is itself a Turing machine, and hence is one of the machines from our list; let us suppose that *X* is really M_k. The self-reference paradoxes we mentioned above—Eubulides' and Russell's—were both triggered by asking a natural question that exposed the latent contradiction. Our proof here employs such a question, and it is this: does *X* halt when it is run on input *k*?

We consider this question as follows. Suppose that *X* halts when it is run on *k*. Then, since we know *X* is really M_k, it follows that M_k halts on *k*; and so, by our construction of *X*, *X* should not halt when it is run on *k*. On the other hand, suppose that *X* does not halt when it is run on *k*. Then, again using the fact that *X* is really M_k, it follows that M_k does not halt on *k*; and so *X* should halt on *k*. So neither outcome is possible—*X* cannot halt on *k*, and it cannot fail to halt on *k*! This is a contradiction, so there cannot be such a machine *X*, and hence there cannot be a Universal Termination Detector *D*.

This style of proof is often referred to as diagonalization, and it was introduced by Cantor to show that one cannot put the real numbers in one-to-one correspondence with the integers. The term "diagonalization" here comes from the following intuition. We imagine drawing an infinite two-dimensional table whose rows correspond to the Turing machines *M1; M2; M3*; . . . and whose columns correspond to all the possible inputs 1; 2; 3; . . . . Each entry of this table—say the entry at the meeting of row *i* and column *j*—indicates whether or not machine M_i halts when it is run on input *j*. Viewed in these terms, our supposed machine *X* "walks down the diagonal" of this table; on input *k*, it consults the table entry at the meeting of row *k* and column *k*, and essentially inverts the answer that it finds there.

Turing machine M and an "undesirable" output n, is there any input that will cause M to produce the output n? But again, from a Code Verifier we could easily build a Termination Detector. No Termination Detector, no Code Verifier.

Suppose you want to verify that the program you've just written will never access a restricted area of memory; or suppose you want to ensure that a certain revision—a transformation of the program—will not cause it to change its behavior. Research in the area of programming languages has developed powerful techniques for program verification and transformation tasks, and they are used effectively to analyze complex programs in practice (Aho and Larus, in Chapter 4, discuss the transformation problem in the context of compiler optimization). Such techniques, however, are developed in a constant struggle against the negative results discussed above: over the years researchers have carved out broader and broader tractable special cases of the problem, but to solve these verification and transformation tasks in their full generality—to perform them correctly on all possible programs—is provably impossible. Such results impose fundamental limitations on our ability to implement and reason about complex pieces of software; they are among the laws that constrain our world.

When Finite Is Not Good Enough

Computers, as we think of them now, did not exist when Turing carried out his seminal work. But by the 1950s and 1960s, as truly automated computation became increasingly available, a growing amount of attention was devoted to the study and development of algorithms—step-by-step computational procedures, made precise by the notion of computability. And as this development began to gather force, it became clear that uncomputability was only one of the laws that constrained our ability to solve problems. The world abounded in problems whose solvability was not in doubt—but for which solving any but the smallest instances seemed practically infeasible.

Some of the most vivid of these problems came from the area of operations research, a field that sprang in large part from the epiphany—conceived during World War II, and spilling into civilian life ever after—that there was a science to the efficient coordinated movement of armies and organizations, the efficient allocation of supplies and raw materials. Thus, we can consider the Traveling Salesman Problem: You are given a map of N cities and the distances between them, as well as a "budget" B; you must visit all the cities via a tour whose total length is at most B. Or consider the Matching Problem: You must pair up $2N$ newly admitted college students—some of whom don't like one another—into N pairs of roommates, so that each pair consists of students who will get along.

In the 1960s, Jack Edmonds came up with a beautiful and efficient algorithm to solve the Matching Problem; and he wrote a paper describing the method. But how should one describe the result, actually? "A computational solution to the Matching Problem"?—this is not quite right, since there's an obvious way to solve it: try all possible pairings, and see if any of them works. There was no question that the Matching Problem had a computable solution in Turing's sense. The crux of the result was in the efficiency of the solution. Jack Edmonds understood this difficulty very clearly: "I am claiming, as a mathematical result, the existence of a good algorithm for finding a . . . matching in a graph. There is an obvious finite algorithm, but that algorithm increases in difficulty exponentially with the size of the graph. It is by no means obvious whether or not there exists an algorithm whose difficulty increases only algebraically with the size of the graph."

It is hard to find much to add to this. There is clearly an algorithm that solves the Matching Problem in a number of steps that is exponential in N—at least N factorial. But try to imagine how long this would take. Even on the fastest computers we have today the problem of forming 30 pairs could require an amount of time comparable to the age of the universe. Yes, the solution is computable; yes, we can even imagine how the whole computation will proceed; but such a method is of no real value to us at all if we are seeking a solution to a problem of even moderate size. We need to find a qualitatively faster method; and this is exactly what Jack Edmonds had accomplished.

Edmonds's concern with "good algorithms" fit naturally into a research agenda that was being pursued contemporaneously by Juris Hartmanis and Richard Stearns—that of determining the intrinsic computational complexity of natural problems, by determining the smallest number of computational steps that are required to produce a solution. And so, following this line of attack, we seek algorithms that require only "polynomial time"—on an input of size N, a "good" algorithm should use a number of steps that is bounded by a polynomial function of N such as N^2 or N^5. Clearly polynomial functions grow much more slowly than exponential ones, and they have a very desirable scaling property—if you increase your input size by a constant multiplicative factor, the running time goes up by a predictable constant factor as well. But however much one tries to justify our interest in polynomial time on theoretical grounds, its primary justification follows the same lines as the Church-Turing thesis that we saw earlier: it accords well with our experience from practice. Problems solvable by polynomial-time algorithms tend overwhelmingly to be efficiently solvable in practice; and for problems that lack polynomial-time algorithms, one tends to encounter enormously difficult instances with some regularity.

The choice of polynomial time as a mathematical surrogate for efficiency has served computer science very well—it has been a powerful guide to the design of good algorithms. And algorithmic efficiency has proved to be a far subtler concept than we could have imagined. Consider again the Traveling Salesman Problem and the Matching Problem. For each, the "search space" is enormous: for the Traveling Salesman, any ordering of the N cities forms a tour that must in principle be considered; for the Matching Problem, any set of pairs that matches all of them is a candidate solution. And yet, despite similarities at this level, their behavior from the point of view of computational difficulty seems to be utterly divergent. Matching has a polynomial-time algorithm, and very large problems are solved every day in practice. For the Traveling Salesman Problem, on the other hand, we are famously without a polynomial-time algorithm, and the solution of relatively small instances can still require a major computational effort.

Where does this enormous difference in computational complexity lie? What features of a computational problem determine its underlying difficulty? The ongoing effort to resolve these questions is a core research activity in computer science today; it has led to a rich theory of computational intractability—including the notion of NP-completeness, which has spread from computer science into the physical, natural, and social sciences. It has also led to the celebrated "P versus NP" question (Box 2.2), which has drawn the attention of mathematicians as well as computer scientists and is now featured on several lists of the foremost open questions in mathematics.

Exponential growth is a recurring theme in computer science, and it is revealing to juxtapose two of its fundamental roles: in Moore's law, which charts the exponential growth in the power of computing machinery (see Hill's essay in this chapter), and in computational complexity, which asserts that the effort needed to solve certain problems grows exponentially in their size. Do these two principles cancel out? If our computing power is growing exponentially over time, will we really be bothered by problems of exponential complexity? The answer is that Moore's law does not make our concerns about exponential complexity go away, and it is important to realize why. The full search space for a 17-city instance of the Traveling Salesman Problem is 16 times larger than the search space for a 16-city instance. So if exhaustively searching the space of solutions for a 16-city problem is at the limit of your current computer's abilities, and if computing power doubles every year and a half, then you'll need to wait 6 years before your new computer can tackle a 17-city problem by brute force—6 years to be able to solve a problem that is only

---

BOX 2.2
Does P Equal NP?

We have been concerned with the set of all problems that can be solved by a polynomial-time algorithm; let's use P to denote this set of problems.

Now, we believe that the Traveling Salesman Problem is very difficult to solve computationally; it is likely that this problem does not belong to the set P we have just defined. But there is at least one good thing we can say about its tractability. Suppose we are given N cities, the distances between them, and a budget B; and suppose that in fact there exists a tour through all these cities of length at most B. Then there exists a way for someone to prove this to us fairly easily: he or she could simply show us the order in which we should visit the cities; we would then tabulate the total distance of this tour and verify that it is at most B.

So the Traveling Salesman Problem may not be efficiently solvable, but it is at least efficiently verifiable: if there is a short tour among the cities we are given, then there exists a "certificate"—the tour itself—that enables us to verify this fact in polynomial time. This is the crux of the Traveling Salesman Problem's complexity, coiled like the "trick" that helps you solve a difficult puzzle: it's hard to find a short tour on your own, but it's easy to be convinced when the short tour is actually revealed to you. This notion of a certificate—the extra piece of information that enables you to verify the answer—can be formalized for computational problems in a general way. As a result, we can consider the set of all problems that are efficiently verifiable in this sense. This is the set NP—the set of all problems for which solutions can be checked (though not necessarily solved) in polynomial time.

It is easy to show that any problem in P must also belong to NP; essentially, this is as easy as arguing that if we can solve a problem on our own in polynomial time, then we can verify any solution in polynomial time as well—even without the help of an additional certificate. But what about the other side of the question: is there a problem that belongs to NP but not to P, a problem for which verifying is easy but solving is hard? Although there is widespread belief that such problems must exist, the issue remains unresolved; this is the famous "P versus NP" question.

To address this question, it is natural to seek out the "hardest" problems in NP, for they are the best candidates for problems that belong to NP but not to P.

---

one city larger! Waiting for Moore's law to deliver better computing power only gets you so far, and it does not beat down the exponential complexity of a deeply intractable problem. What is needed is not just better hardware on which to apply brute force, but also a better algorithm for finding a solution—something like what Edmonds found for the Matching Problem.

The fact that simply-stated problems can have enormous complexity, with solutions that are computationally very difficult to find, has led to new perspectives on a number of well-studied ideas. Cryptography has

How can we formalize the notion that one problem is at least as hard as another? The answer lies in reducibility, an idea that came up implicitly when we discussed computational impossibility. We say that a problem A is "reducible" to a problem B if, given a "black box" capable of solving instances of B in polynomial time, we can design a polynomial-time algorithm for A. In other words, we are able to solve A by drawing on a solution to B as a "resource." It follows that if we actually had a polynomial-time algorithm for problem B, we could use this as our "black box," and hence design a polynomial-time algorithm for problem A. Or, simply running this reasoning backward, if there is no polynomial-time algorithm for A, then there cannot be a polynomial-time algorithm for B: problem B is at least as hard as problem A.

So here is a natural thing we might search for: a single problem B in NP with the property that every problem in NP is reducible to B. Such a problem would, quite conclusively, be among the hardest problems in NP—a solution to it would imply a solution to everything in NP. But do such problems exist? Why should there be a single problem that is this powerful?

In the early 1970s, Steve Cook in North America and Leonid Levin in the Soviet Union independently made the crucial breakthrough, discovering a number of natural problems in NP with precisely this property: everything in NP can be reduced to them. Today we say that such a problem is "NP-complete," and research over the past decades has led to the discovery that there are literally thousands of natural NP-complete problems, across all the sciences. For example, determining the winner(s) under a wide variety of election and auction schemes is NP-complete. Optimizing the layout of the gates in a computer chip is NP-complete. Finding the folding of minimum energy for discrete models of proteins is NP-complete. The Traveling Salesman Problem—the tough nut that started us on this road—is NP-complete. And an important thing to bear in mind is this: because every problem in NP is reducible to any of these, they are all reducible to each other. There is a polynomial-time algorithm for one if and only if there is a polynomial-time algorithm for all. So we have come to realize that researchers in a host of different areas, struggling over a spectrum of computationally intractable problems, have in a fairly precise sense all been struggling over the same problem; this is the great insight that NP-completeness has given us. The original question remains open.

been revolutionized by the theory of complexity, for the design of secure communication protocols is a field that exists in a mirror-world where difficult computational problems—codes that are easy to apply and hard to break—are resources to be cultivated (see Sudan in Chapter 7). The RSA public-key cryptosystem was inspired by the presumed difficulty of factoring large integers, with the prime factors of a number N forming the hidden "key" whose knowledge allows for easy decryption. The age-old notion of randomness—a concept that is intuitively apparent but notoriously tricky to define—has been given an appealing formalization based on computational complexity: a sequence of digits appears "random" to an observer if it is computationally difficult for the observer to predict the next digit with odds significantly better than guessing.

For designers of algorithms, we have seen that their struggle with the complexity of computation has proceeded at a number of different levels. One boundary divides the computable from the uncomputable—it is feasible to build a step-by-step interpreter for computer programs, but one cannot design an algorithm that decides whether arbitrary programs will terminate. Another boundary divides polynomial-time solvability from the exponential growth of brute-force search. But while polynomial time is indeed a good high-level means for gauging computational tractability, there are an increasing number of applications, typically involving very large datasets, where simply having a polynomial-time algorithm is far from adequate. Suppose the size of the input is measured in terabytes (millions of megabytes); an algorithm that takes a number of steps equal to the cube of the input size is no more useful in practice than one that never terminates.

None of this is to say that polynomial time has lost its relevance to the design of algorithms. But for many large-scale problems, we are faced with a reprise of the situation in the 1950s and 1960s, when we tumbled from a concern with computability to a concern with computational complexity: as our real-world computational needs expand, our guidelines for what constitutes an "acceptable" algorithm become increasingly stringent. And this in turn has led to new lines of research, focusing for example on algorithms that must run in time very close to the size of the input itself; algorithms that must "stream" through the input data in one pass, unable to store significant parts of it for post-processing.

While algorithm design has deepened into the study of increasingly time-efficient techniques, it has also opened outward, revealing that running time is just one of many sources of complexity that must be faced. In many applications—scheduling under real-time conditions, or managing a busy network—the input is not a static object but a dynamic one, with new data arriving continuously over time. Decisions must be made and solutions must be constructed adaptively, without knowledge of future input. In other applications, the computation is distributed over many processors, and one seeks algorithms that require as little communication, and synchronization, as possible. And through all these settings, from NP-complete problems onward, algorithms have been increasingly designed and analyzed with the understanding that the optimal solution may be unattainable, and that the optimum may have to serve only as an implicit benchmark against which the quality of the algorithm's solution can be measured.

The Lens of Computation

Our contemplation of computation has led us quickly to the "P versus NP" question, now considered among the deepest open problems in mathematics and computer science. More recently, our views on complexity have been influenced by the striking confluence of computation and quantum physics: What happens to our standard notions of running time and complexity when the computation unfolds according to the principles of quantum mechanics? It is now known that access to such a hypothetical "quantum computer" would yield polynomial-time algorithms for certain problems (including integer factorization and the breaking of the RSA cryptosystem) that are believed to be intractable on standard computers. What are the ultimate limits of quantum computers? And are there theoretical obstacles to building them (in addition to the practical ones currently braved in labs all over the world)? These questions, purely computational in their origin, present some of the most daunting challenges facing theoretical physics today.

Biology is a field where the synergy with computation seems to go ever deeper the more we look. Let us leave aside all the ways in which sophisticated algorithmic ideas are transforming the practice of biology with vast genomic and structural databases, massive numerical simulations of molecules, and the fearsome symbol-crunching of the Human Genome Project. Instead, consider how we might view molecular biology itself through a computational lens, with the cell as an information-processing engine. For fundamentally, a biological system like a cell is simply a chemical system in which the information content is explicit. The genome is part of the overall chemical system, but it is not there to take part in the chemistry itself; rather, it is there as a sophisticated encoding of the chemical processes that will take place. It is a programming abstraction—it is the representation of the real thing, co-existing with the thing itself.

Just as computation distinguishes itself from the rest of technology, so are biological systems intrinsically different from all other physical and chemical systems—for they too have separated the application from the device. We can take a cell and change a few symbols in its genome—splice in a new gene or two—and we can cause its chemistry to change completely. We have replaced one piece of code with another; the device—the cellular hardware—has been left alone, while we simply changed the application running on it. This phenomenon really seems to have no parallel in the other sciences. Surely, the non-biological world obeys fundamental laws, but it does not contain—and actually implement—an explicit representation of these laws. Where in the solar system are the few molecules, encoding the laws of gravity and motion, which we could modify to cause the planets to follow more eccentric orbits?

Computation as a technology that follows its own laws; computation as the quintessence of universality; computation as a powerful perspective on the world and on science—these are issues that still drive our study of the phenomenon today. And the more we grapple with the underlying principles of computation, the more we see their reflections and imprints on all disciplines—in the way structured tasks can be cast as stylized computational activities; in the surprising complexity of simple systems; and in the rich and organic interplay between information and code.

PLATE 1 Computer-generated water being poured into a glass.

PLATE 2 A ball making a splash in a tank of computer-generated water.

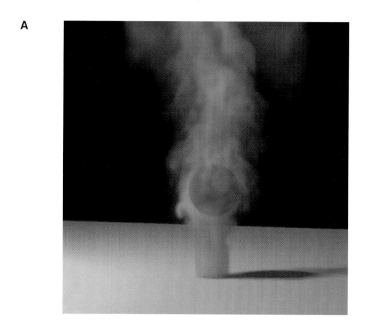

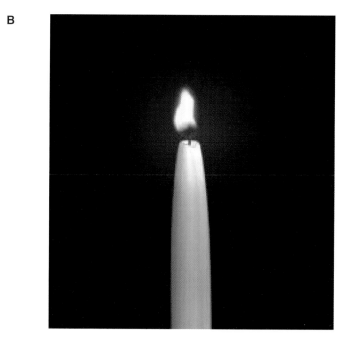

PLATE 3 Computer-generated smoke rolls past a sphere (a) and a computer-generated candle flame (b).

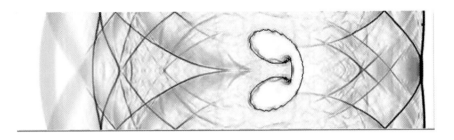

PLATE 4 Computer simulation of a shock wave impinging on a Helium bubble.

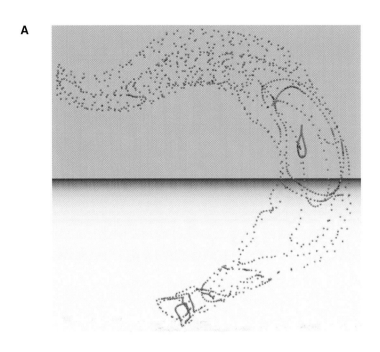

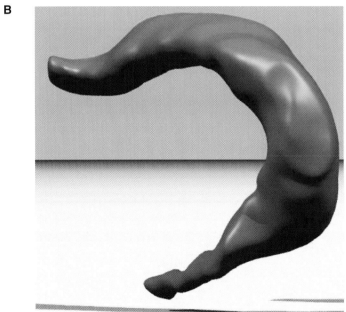

PLATE 5 (a) MRI data points from a rat's brain and (b) computer reconstruction of the brain geometry.

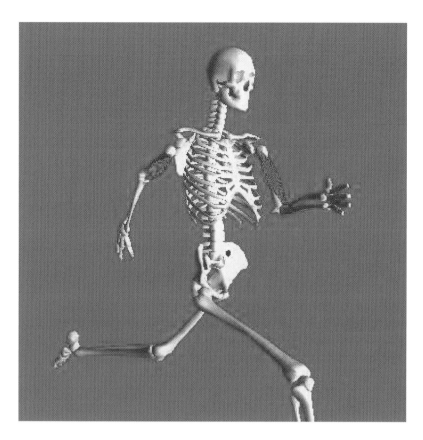

PLATE 6 Computer simulation of a running skeleton with biceps.

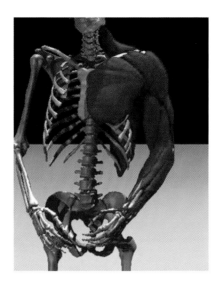

PLATE 7 A tetrahedral muscle mesh ready for finite element simulation.

PLATE 8 Computer simulation of a piece of draped cloth.

QUANTUM INFORMATION PROCESSING

Charles H. Bennett, IBM Research

Computer science is based on a very fruitful abstraction whose roots are as old as mathematics but whose power was fully appreciated only in the 20th century: the notion that information and computation are a worthwhile object of study in their own right, independent of the physical apparatus used to carry the information or perform the computation. While at the most obvious level, Moore's law (see Hill in this chapter) is a hardware success story, this success has only been possible because information is such an abstract stuff: make a bit a thousand times smaller and it remains useful for the same purposes as before, unlike a thousand-fold smaller car or potato.

Although Moore's law has survived many early predictions of its demise, no exponential growth can go on forever. The present few decades are clearly an exceptional time in the history of computing. Sooner or later something will have to give, since at the present rate of shrinkage, information technology will reach atomic dimensions within 20 years. Accordingly, considerable thought and long-range planning are already being devoted to the challenges of designing and fabricating devices at the atomic scale and getting them to work reliably, a field broadly known as nanotechnology. However, it has long been known that atoms and other tiny objects obey laws of quantum physics that in many respects defy common sense. For example, observing an atom disturbs its motion, while not observing it allows it to spread out and behave as if it were in several different places at the same time. Until recently, computer designers considered such quantum effects mostly as a nuisance that would cause small devices to be less reliable and more error-prone than their larger cousins.

What is new, and what makes quantum informatics a coherent discipline, rather than a vexing set of technological problems, is the realization that quantum effects are not just a nuisance; rather, they offer a new and more comprehensive way of thinking about information, which can be exploited to perform important and otherwise impossible information-processing tasks. Already they have been used to create unconditionally secure cryptographic key agreement protocols, and in the future, if a quantum computer can be built, it could easily perform some computations (most notably the factorization of large numbers) that would take longer than the age of the universe by the best known algorithms, not only on today's supercomputers, but also on the supercomputers of 2050 (by which time we predict Moore's law will have ended).

The way in which quantum effects can speed up computation is not a simple quantitative improvement, such as would result from using a faster processor, or some fixed number of parallel processors to speed up computations by some constant factor depending on the hardware. Rather it is a qualitative improvement in the functional form of the computation cost, similar to what one typically gets by discovering a smarter algorithm to solve a problem that previously seemed hard. With quantum information processing the physical form of information, for the first time, has a qualitative bearing on the efficiency with which it can be processed, and the things that can be done with it. Quantum computers do not speed up all computations equally: a few, like factoring, are sped up super-polynomially; general NP search problems like the Traveling Salesman Problem are sped up quadratically, while other problems are not sped up at all.

But to say quantum computers offer the hope of using physical effects to dramatically speed up some computations is putting things backwards. In hindsight, it should rather be said that the laws of quantum physics, which as far as we know today apply to everything in the universe, provide a more powerful arsenal of physically performable mathematical operations than Turing imagined when he formalized the notion of a computer. Availing ourselves of this more powerful arsenal, although it does not enlarge the class of computable functions, makes some computational problems qualitatively easier than they seemed before. Unlike the former hope of a qualitative speedup from analog processing, which has largely been dashed by the ability of digital computers, via discrete approximation to simulate analog processes more accurately than they can be reproducibly performed in nature, quantum computation offers a realistic hope of qualitatively enlarging the scope of feasible computation.

However, it should be noted that actually building a useful quantum computer presents formidable technical challenges, which will probably be overcome eventually, but not any time soon. The confidence that these obstacles can ultimately be overcome rests largely on the theory of quantum error correction and fault tolerance, developed since 1995. This theory, which is analogous to the classical theory of fault tolerance developed by von Neumann and others in the days when computers were made of vacuum tubes and relays, allows arbitrarily large reliable quantum computations to be done on imperfect hardware, provided the hardware exceeds some threshold of reliability. The technical problem is that the quantum threshold is higher than the classical threshold discovered by von Neumann, while today's quantum computing hardware processes quantum information far less reliably than vacuum tubes process classical information, so there remains a gap of several orders of magnitude that still needs to be closed. There is every reason to believe it can be closed, but how and when remain to be seen.

Just how do quantum information and the hardware used to process it differ from the ordinary classical type of information processing formalized by Turing? States of a Turing machine tape, or any other digital storage medium, are in principle reliably distinguishable, and the tape can be copied accurately without disturbing it. This is a reasonable idealization of the behavior of macroscopic information processing hardware like punch cards, electromechanical relays, and even today's most advanced microprocessors and memory chips. But it has been known since the early 20th century that at an atomic and subatomic scale actual matter behaves more subtly: not all states are reliably distinguishable even in principle, and information stored in such states cannot be copied without disturbing it. Speaking metaphorically, quantum information is like the information in a dream: attempting to describe your dream to someone else changes your memory of it, so you begin to forget the dream and remember only what you said about it.

This dreamlike behavior notwithstanding, quantum information obeys exact and well-understood laws. The so-called *superposition principle* holds that the possible states of any physical system correspond to directions in a d-dimensional space ("Hilbert space"), where the dimension d is characteristic of the system and represents the system's maximum number of reliably distinguishable states. Two states are reliably distinguishable if and only if their Hilbert space directions are orthogonal (as is usually the case with macroscopic systems). Physically implementable operations on the system always conserve or reduce distinguishability, corresponding roughly to rigid rotations and projections in the Hilbert space. In the simplest nontrivial case $d = 2$ and the system (e.g., the internal state of an electron or photon, for example) is called a *qubit*. If two reliably distinguishable states of the qubit (e.g., horizontal and vertical polarizations for a photon) are arbitrarily designated |0> and |1>, a general state may be expressed as a linear combination $\alpha|0> + \beta|1>$, where α and β are complex numbers such that $|\alpha|^2 + |\beta|^2 = 1$. Another quantum principle, the *projection postulate*, holds that if a qubit in this state is subjected to an observation that would reliably distinguish |0> from |1>, the qubit behaves like |0> with probability $|\alpha|^2$ and like |1> with probability $|\beta|^2$. Observing the system again yields no new information: the system again behaves like |0> or |1> according to the result of the first observation. More generally, observing a quantum system causes it to behave probabilistically, losing information about its previous state, except when the system was already in one of the states the observation was designed to distinguish. The art of quantum computing consists of accurately preparing the quantum computer in a desired initial state, performing a sequence of accurately controlled manipulations (rotations) of its state *without* observing it during the intermediate stages of the computation, and then finally observing the final state to obtain a useful output.

This may sound a lot like analog computation, which is not believed to be significantly more powerful than conventional digital computation. How, one might ask, can a qubit—say a photon, which may be polarized at an arbitrary angle θ relative to the horizontal—be more powerful than an analog system—say a mechanical wheel oriented at angle θ relative to some standard position? At first sight, the wheel would appear more powerful. Not only can its orientation be accurately manipulated, but also the orientation (unlike a photon's) can be observed quite precisely without significantly disturbing it. The essential difference, which makes quantum computation more powerful than analog computation, comes from the way individual information-bearing subsystems (e.g., qubits) combine to form a larger system (e.g., a quantum register, or a whole quantum computer). An n qubit register has 2^n reliably distinguishable states corresponding to the n-bit strings $|000...\rangle$ through $|111...1\rangle$; more generally the Hilbert space of a compound quantum system has a dimensionality equal to the *product* of the Hilbert space dimensions of its parts. By the superposition principle, the general state of an n qubit register corresponds to a direction in a 2^n dimensional space; and during the computation the state may undergo controlled rotations in this large space. By contrast, an n wheel analog computer's state lives in a parameter space of only n dimensions; more generally, an analog system's parameter space has a dimensionality equal to the *sum* of the dimensionalities of its parts. The quantum computer's advantage comes from its enormously larger state space. However, the advantage is rather subtle, because at the end of a quantum computation, in order to get a classical output, it is necessary to make an observation, and, by the projection postulate, doing so collapses the 2^n parameter quantum state back down to n classical bits. This severe bottleneck at the end of the computation means that an n qubit quantum computer cannot process any greater volume of information than an n bit classical computer. However, for some computations, it can do the processing in far fewer steps because of the extra maneuvering room the large Hilbert space provides during intermediate stages of the computation.

As noted earlier, the big technical barrier to be overcome in constructing a quantum computer is to make the rate of hardware errors, during the unobserved portion of the computation preceding the final observation, sufficiently small. This is qualitatively similar to the problem digital computers faced in the era of vacuum tubes and relays, but quantitatively worse, because a quantum computer needs to be isolated much more carefully from its environment to attain a given level of reliability. In particular, because of the disturbing effect of observation on quantum systems, quantum computers must be designed to prevent information about the data being processed from leaking out of the computer into the environment before the end of the computation. (If such premature leakage took place, the computation would begin to behave like a classical probabilistic computation instead of a quantum one, and the advantages of quantum speedup would be lost.) Fortunately the formalism of quantum error correction and fault tolerance allows arbitrarily good protection against such leakage to be achieved, provided the basic hardware exceeds some finite threshold of reliability.

Aside from computation per se, quantum information science includes the disciplines of quantum communication and quantum cryptography. The latter field is at a far more mature stage of development than is quantum computation per se, with successful laboratory experiments and even a few startup companies. Quantum cryptography is based on the fact that eavesdropping on quantum systems disturbs them. In a typical implementation, a random sequence of N faint polarized light pulses is sent through an optical fiber, after which the sender and receiver, by public discussion of the sent and received signals, estimate the amount of disturbance and hence of potential eavesdropping. If it is too great, they abort the protocol. Otherwise they can proceed to derive from the sent and received signals a shorter sequence of random secret key bits on which the eavesdropper has arbitrarily little information. More precisely it can be shown that any eavesdropping strategy obeying the laws of quantum physics, even when assisted by unlimited computing power, yields only exponentially little expected information on the final key sequence, if any. The eavesdropper thus faces the dilemma of eavesdropping gently and learning essentially nothing, or eavesdropping strongly and causing the protocol to abort. Quantum cryptography is practical because it does not require a full fledged quantum computer, only classical computers supplemented by equipment for generating, transporting, and detecting quantum signals, all of which are available today. Unlike classical methods of key agreement, it is unconditionally secure, and thus impervious to future improvements in algorithms or computing power.

Although it was inspired by physics, quantum information processing is a mathematically coherent and well-characterized extension of classical information processing. Indeed the latter can now best be viewed as a useful but limited subset of the larger subject of quantum information processing, somewhat as the real numbers are a useful but limited subset of the complex numbers. To continue the analogy, quantum information processing provides solutions, or improved solutions, to some problems in classical computation and cryptography, just as the complex plane provides solutions and insights into problems in real analysis not explicitly involving complex variables. For this reason, even aside from its technological implications, quantum informatics is an intellectually exciting discipline, with far-reaching implications for the basic mathematical and physical sciences, both theoretical and experimental. It is already providing new ways of thinking about a wide variety of scientific and technical questions, and has begun to affect how science is taught, in a way that will bring a deeper understanding of the fruitful abstraction that is information not only to computer scientists but also to a broad segment of the lay public.

For further information:

- Jozef Gruska, *Quantum Computing* (McGraw-Hill, 1999, ISBN 007 709503 0)
- Michael Nielsen and Isaac L. Chuang, *Quantum Computation and Quantum Information* (Cambridge University Press, 2000, ISBN 0 0521 63235 8)
- U.S. National Science Foundation report on quantum information science: http://www.nsf.gov/pubs/2000/nsf00101/nsf00101.htm
- Online course notes: http://www.theory.caltech.edu/%7Epreskill/ph219/ http://www.cs.berkeley.edu/~vazirani/qc.html
- Other quantum information Web sites: http://www.research.ibm.com/quantuminfo/ http://www.iro.umontreal.ca/labs/theorique/index.html.en http://www.qubit.org/

3

Simulation

I n Chapter 2, the essay by Kleinberg and Papadimitriou discusses the
universality of computers. To exploit this universality, we must specialize the computing engine to a specific task. This specialization
ultimately takes the form of a program, but the program does not appear
by magic—its creator needs to understand the task deeply. Further, a
program must handle all variants of the task, not just those that the programmer can imagine. Usually we address this challenge by creating a
model of the task's problem domain. The model may be expressed in many
different ways, but it can be understood in isolation from any particular
program that implements it. These models may be designed to match
physical reality, or they may express alternative sets of laws. In this way,
simulation allows computer scientists—and others—to explain phenomena
that may be difficult, dangerous, or impossible to explore in reality.

The use of digital computer simulations for scientific research is half a
century old. Strogatz reflects on the explanatory power of Fermi's early
simulations and their profound effects. These early models of nonlinear
systems gave better insight into the underlying phenomena than either
the physical experiments (which proceeded too fast) or the math (which
was too hard for the times).

Fedkiw describes the modern analog of Fermi's experiments—the use
of simulation to visualize complex phenomena such as turbulent flow. He
shows how this mode of research complements the use of experiments
and closed-form mathematics.

THE REAL SCIENTIFIC HERO OF 1953

Steven Strogatz, Cornell University

NOTE: Originally published in the *New York Times*,
this op-ed appeared on March 4, 2003.
Reprinted by permission of the author.

Last week newspapers and magazines devoted tens of thousands of words to the 50th anniversary of the discovery of the chemical structure of DNA. While James D. Watson and Francis Crick certainly deserved a good party, there was no mention of another scientific feat that also turned 50 this year—one whose ramifications may ultimately turn out to be as profound as those of the double helix.

In 1953, Enrico Fermi and two of his colleagues at Los Alamos Scientific Laboratory, John Pasta and Stanislaw Ulam, invented the concept of a "computer experiment." Suddenly the computer became a telescope for the mind, a way of exploring inaccessible processes like the collision of black holes or the frenzied dance of subatomic particles—phenomena that are too large or too fast to be visualized by traditional experiments, and too complex to be handled by pencil-and-paper mathematics. The computer experiment offered a third way of doing science. Over the past 50 years, it has helped scientists to see the invisible and imagine the inconceivable.

Fermi and his colleagues introduced this revolutionary approach to better understand entropy, the tendency of all systems to decay to states of ever greater disorder. To observe the predicted descent into chaos in unprecedented detail, Fermi and his team created a virtual world, a simulation taking place inside the circuits of an electronic behemoth known as Maniac, the most powerful supercomputer of its era. Their test problem involved a deliberately simplified model of a vibrating atomic lattice, consisting of 64 identical particles (representing atoms) linked end to end by springs (representing the chemical bonds between them).

This structure was akin to a guitar string, but with an unfamiliar feature: normally, a guitar string behaves "linearly"—pull it to the side and it pulls back, pull it twice as far and it pulls back twice as hard. Force and response are proportional. In the 300 years since Isaac Newton invented calculus, mathematicians and physicists had mastered the analysis of systems like that, where causes are strictly proportional to effects, and the whole is exactly equal to the sum of the parts.

But that's not how the bonds between real atoms behave. Twice the stretch does not produce exactly twice the force. Fermi suspected that this nonlinear character of chemical bonds might be the key to the inevitable increase of entropy. Unfortunately, it also made the mathematics impenetrable. A nonlinear system like this couldn't be analyzed by breaking it into pieces. Indeed, that's the hallmark of a nonlinear system: the parts don't add up to the whole. Understanding a system like this defied all known methods. It was a mathematical monster.

Undaunted, Fermi and his collaborators plucked their virtual string and let Maniac grind away, calculating hundreds of simultaneous interactions, updating all the forces and positions, marching the virtual string forward in time in a series of slow-motion snapshots. They expected to see its shape degenerate into a random vibration, the musical counterpart of which would be a meaningless hiss, like static on the radio.

What the computer revealed was astonishing. Instead of a hiss, the string played an eerie tune, almost like music from an alien civilization. Starting from a pure tone, it progressively added a series of overtones, replacing one with another, gradually changing the timbre. Then it suddenly reversed direction, deleting overtones in the opposite sequence, before finally returning almost precisely to the original tone. Even creepier, it repeated this strange melody again and again, indefinitely, but always with subtle variations on the theme.

Fermi loved this result—he referred to it affectionately as a "little discovery." He had never guessed that nonlinear systems could harbor such a penchant for order.

In the 50 years since this pioneering study, scientists and engineers have learned to harness nonlinear systems, making use of their capacity for self-organization. Lasers, now used everywhere from eye surgery to checkout scanners, rely on trillions of atoms emitting light waves in unison. Superconductors transmit electrical current without resistance, the byproduct of billions of pairs of electrons marching in lockstep. The resulting technology has spawned the world's most sensitive detectors, used by doctors to pinpoint diseased tissues in the brains of epileptics without the need for invasive surgery, and by geologists to locate oil buried deep underground.

But perhaps the most important lesson of Fermi's study is how feeble even the best minds are at grasping the dynamics of large, nonlinear systems. Faced with a thicket of interlocking feedback loops, where everything affects everything else, our familiar ways of thinking fall apart. To solve the most important problems of our time, we're going to have to change the way we do science.

For example, cancer will not be cured by biologists working alone. Its solution will require a melding of both great discoveries of 1953. Many cancers, perhaps most of them, involve the derangement of biochemical networks that choreograph the activity of thousands of genes and proteins. As Fermi and his colleagues taught us, a complex system like this can't be understood merely by cataloging its parts and the rules governing their interactions. The nonlinear logic of cancer will be fathomed only through the collaborative efforts of molecular biologists—the heirs to Dr. Watson and Dr. Crick—and mathematicians who specialize in complex systems, the heirs to Fermi, Pasta, and Ulam.

Can such an alliance take place? Well, it can if scientists embrace the example set by an unstoppable 86-year-old who, following his co-discovery of the double helix, became increasingly interested in computer simulations of complex systems in the brain.

Happy anniversary, Dr. Crick. And a toast to the memory of Enrico Fermi.

MAKING A COMPUTATIONAL SPLASH

Ronald Fedkiw, Stanford University

Have you ever sat in a movie theater with a box of popcorn and a soft drink watching a movie like *The Perfect Storm* and wondered where Hollywood found a cameraman brave enough to operate a camera under such dangerous conditions? Well, that particular cameraman was sitting in a small office north of San Francisco at a company called Industrial Light and Magic, which was founded in 1975 by George Lucas of *Star Wars* fame. There, a computer graphics specialist, our "cameraman," safely operated the camera with the mouse attached to his computer. In fact, the camera was little more than a computer program that calculated the relative positions of boats and waves in order to add captivating imagery to a tale about fishermen struggling with treacherous waves on rough seas. Hollywood films are created to captivate and entertain, and thus they frequently contain exciting scenes with natural phenomena such as water waves, smoke, tornados, or even lava erupting from volcanoes. Obviously, we're not going to put George Clooney on a boat in the middle of the Atlantic Ocean and subsequently pulverize it with waves until it sinks. In fact, we're not going to put anyone on a boat in such a treacherous storm, assuming we could even find such a storm in the first place. It turns out to be a lot easier to make waves out of math than out of water.

For centuries, applied mathematicians and physicists have derived mathematical equations describing the behavior of a variety of substances including water waves in the ocean and the metal hull of a ship (Box 3.1). These equations are quite complicated and can be solved only in special situations or with the aid of simplifying assumptions that usually rule out problems of practical interest. However, in the last half century, the advent of computer technology has led to a revolution in the study of these types of equations. Using approximation theory, numerical analysts have devised a number of algorithms that enable one to program computers to estimate solutions to many of the equations governing the physical world to any desired accuracy. Moreover, these numerical solutions provide useful information for practical problems of interest to both scientists and engineers.

Solving such problems falls into an area of research referred to as "scientific computing." Scientific computing has become the third branch of research in many engineering departments, joining theory and experiment as classical approaches to obtaining information about the world around us. While scientific computing has classically been applied to physical problems such as those faced in mechanical, aerospace, and struc-

BOX 3.1
The Equations That Describe the Movement of Liquids and Gases

The mathematical equations that describe the movement of liquids and gases are known as the Navier-Stokes equations. These equations describe how fluid particles move through space, the effects of internal friction or viscosity, and the way sound waves are transmitted through a fluid. While viscosity is relatively straightforward to account for, the particle motion and sound wave transmission can be rather difficult to deal with. Computational methods for approximating these effects have to determine which way the particles and the sound waves are moving (and they usually move in different directions) and account for both this directionality and the speed of propagation. When modeling high-speed gas flows containing shock waves as shown in Plate 4, it is important to accurately resolve both the particle motion and the sound wave transmission effects. On the other hand, when modeling sloshing water or other liquids as shown in Plates 1 and 2, precise treatment of the sound waves is not necessary in order to obtain adequate solutions of the equations. Moreover, the treatment of fast-moving sound waves would make the problem computationally much more expensive to solve. To remedy this difficulty, liquids can be assumed to be incompressible; that is, they preserve volume. This assumption removes the directional component and the stiffness of the sound waves, making the problem computationally tractable. Moreover, this is a physically realistic assumption for liquids, especially when one considers that a liquid's resistance to compression is responsible for the strong forces produced by hydraulics devices.

tural engineering, the fastest growing application areas may currently be in electrical and computer engineering and in biology and medicine. More broadly, scientific computing encompasses both computational science and computational mathematics. We emphasize that mathematics is the fundamental language for problem solving, and when confronted with a problem most scientific researchers attempt to formulate a mathematical description of that problem. Once the mathematical description exists, the problem is potentially solvable on a computer using either existing algorithmic techniques or newly devised methods. Thus, scientific computing has become a fundamental requirement for solving problems in signal processing, image analysis, robotics, computer vision, human computer interaction, and computer graphics.

Returning to our cameraman and his goal of captivating us with dramatic sequences of waves pounding on a small ship, we now see that there are a lot of potential resources for creating "special effects" waves on the computer. In the particular case of *The Perfect Storm*, Industrial Light and Magic (ILM) had recently hired a professor of atmospheric science (who specializes in scientific computing) to use his knowledge of oceans and waves, especially his algorithmic knowledge, to construct numerical solutions of large crashing waves on the ILM computers.

The Perfect Storm was not the first instance of scientific computing algorithms being used to make movies of boats and waves. A few years earlier, a Department of Defense (DOD)-oriented company called Areté Associates started a small spin-off company called Areté Entertainment to create computer graphics software that constructs artificial, but surprisingly realistic, ocean wave models. One can imagine that it could be particularly useful to be able to reproduce ocean wave models based on, for example, current wind speeds. If one could measure the wind and estimate what the ocean wave pattern should look like, this could be compared to the actual wave patterns in order to ascertain if there have been any recent outside influences on the wave patterns. That is, one could subtract the estimated wave pattern from the current wave pattern, thus revealing the wake of a large ship that passed through the water even some time ago. This becomes a lot more interesting when one realizes that underwater ships (submarines) can create surface disturbances as well. The implications for to the surveillance community are obvious. Using its knowledge of scientific computing algorithms for studying waves, Areté Entertainment developed computer graphics software to create ocean waves based on wind speeds. This software has won numerous awards and was used to create ocean waves in many films such as *Water World* and James Cameron's *Titanic*. Another recent film, *Cast Away*, used similar technology to simulate a plane crashing into the ocean, stranding Tom Hanks on a deserted island.

As mentioned earlier, scientific computing algorithms can be used to simulate a variety of natural phenomena, including the water shown in Plates 1 and 2, and the smoke and fire shown in Plate 3. While these everyday events (smoke, fire, and water) are easy to relate to, similar numerical techniques can also be applied to events that the human eye will miss completely. For example, Plate 4 shows a computer simulation of a high-speed shock wave interacting with a bubble of helium. Scientific computing is having a growing impact in the fields of imaging and data analysis as well. This is important, for example, in medicine, biology, and even surveillance. For example, Plate 5 shows several data points obtained from MRI imaging of a rat's brain along with a three-dimensional geometric reconstruction of the rat brain obtained by using numerical methods on a computer.

Possibly the most exciting area for future applications of scientific computing is the computer simulation and study of humans themselves. Researchers in biomechanics and medicine are currently working to write down mathematical equations and numerical models that describe most of the human body from the cardiovascular system to muscles, bones, and organs. As these equations and models are formulated, there is an ever-growing need for new computational algorithms that can be used for the computer simulation of biological structures. Plate 6 shows a sample computer simulation of a skeleton running. Geometric models were used for the bones, mathematical equations were used to describe the limited motion allowed for by the connective tissue in joints, and special models for soft tissue were used to simulate the muscles (the red regions in Plate 6 represent the biceps muscles). Plate 7 shows 30 muscles of the upper limb represented as a tetrahedral mesh ready for finite element simulation. Computer simulation of humans is of interest to a wide variety of commercial industries as well. The entertainment industry would like to simulate virtual actors, the textile industry would like to simulate both runway models and everyday customers trying on virtual clothing, and so on. See Plate 8 for a computer simulation of a piece of draped cloth.

As both everyday personal computers and national laboratory super-computers continue to increase in speed and as better algorithms are developed, the size, complexity, and realism of the problems that can be simulated on these computers increase as well. In addition, as researchers branch out into new and exciting research areas, they will formulate mathematical descriptions of their problems that are subsequently amenable to computer simulation. The future is bright in a number of research areas, and where researchers go, math and computer algorithms are sure to follow.

4

Abstraction, Representation, and Notations

M odels capture phenomena—of the world or of the imagination—in such a way that a general-purpose computer can emulate, simulate, or create the phenomena. But the models are usually not obvious. The real world is complex and nonlinear, there's too much detail to deal with, and relationships among the details are often hidden. Computer scientists deal with this problem by careful, deliberate creation of abstractions that express the models. These abstractions are represented symbolically, in notations appropriate to the phenomena. The design of languages for these models and for analyzing, processing, and executing them is a core activity of computer science.

Indeed, abstraction is a quintessential activity of computer science—the intellectual tool that allows computer scientists to express their understanding of a problem, manage complexity, and select the level of detail and degree of generality they need at the moment. Computer scientists create and discard abstractions as freely as engineers and architects create and discard design sketches.

Shaw describes the role of abstraction in building software, both the stuff of programs—algorithms and representations—and the role that specification and formal reasoning play in developing those abstractions. Specific software-design techniques such as information hiding and hierarchical organization provide ways to organize the abstract definitions and the information they control. Aho and Larus describe how programming languages provide a notation to encode abstractions so as to allow their direct execution by computer.

ABSTRACTION: IMPOSING ORDER ON COMPLEXITY
IN SOFTWARE DESIGN

Mary Shaw, Carnegie Mellon University

The success of a complex designed system depends on the correct organization and interaction of thousands, even millions, of individual parts. If the designer must reason about all the parts at once, the complexity of the design task often overwhelms human capability. Software designers, like other designers, manage this complexity by separating the design task into relatively independent parts. Often, this entails designing large systems as hierarchical collections of subsystems, with the subsystems further decomposed into sub-subsystems, and so on until the individual components are of manageable size.

For typical consumer products, the subsystems are physical components that can be put together on assembly lines. But the principle of hierarchical system organization does not require an assembly line. Simon[1] tells a parable of two watchmakers, Hora and Tempus. Both made excellent watches and were often visited by their customers. Their watches were similar, each with about 1000 parts, but Hora prospered while Tempus became progressively poorer and eventually lost his shop. Tempus, it seems, made his watches in such a way that a partially assembled watch fell apart any time he put it down to deal with an interruption. Hora, on the other hand, made stable subassemblies of about 10 parts and assembled these into 10 larger assemblies, then joined these to make each watch. So any time one of the watchmakers was interrupted by a customer, Tempus had to restart from scratch on the current watch, but Hora only lost the work of the current 10-unit assembly—a small fraction of Tempus' loss.

Software systems do not require manual assembly of parts, but they are large, complex, and amenable to a similar sort of discipline. Software design benefits from hierarchical system organization based on subsystems that are relatively independent and that have known, simple, interactions. Software designers create conceptual subassemblies with coherent, comprehensible capabilities, similar to Hora's subassemblies. But whereas Hora's subassemblies might have been selected for convenience and physical organization, computer scientists are more likely to create structure around concepts and responsibilities. In doing so they can often state the idea, or *abstraction*, that is realized by the structure; for example, the capabilities of a software component are often described in

---

[1]Herbert A. Simon, 1997, *Sciences of the Artificial*, 3rd Ed., MIT Press, Cambridge, Mass., pp. 188ff.

terms of the component's observable properties, rather than the details of the component's implementation. While these abstractions may correspond to discrete software components (the analog of physical parts), this is not necessarily the case. So, for example, a computer scientist might create an abstraction for the software that computes a satellite trajectory but might equally well create an abstraction for a communication protocol whose implementation is woven through all the separate software components of a system. Indeed, the abstractions of computer science can be used in non-hierarchical as well as hierarchical structures. The abstractions of computer science are not in general the grand theories of the sciences (though we have those as well; see Kleinberg and Papadimitriou in Chapter 2), but rather specific conceptual units designed for specific tasks.

We represent these software abstractions in a combination of notations—the descriptive notations of specifications, the imperative notations of programming, the descriptive notations of diagrams, and even narrative prose. This combination of descriptive and imperative languages provides separate descriptions of *what* is to be done (the specification) and *how* it is to be done (the implementation). A software component corresponding to an abstraction has a descriptive (sometimes formal) specification of its abstract capabilities, an operational (usually imperative) definition of its implementation, and some assurance—with varying degrees of rigor and completeness—that the specification is consistent with the implementation. Formal descriptive notations, in particular, have evolved more or less together with operational notations, and progress with each depends on progress with the other. The result is that we can design large-scale systems software purposefully, rather than through pure virtuosity, craft, or blind luck. We have not achieved—indeed, may never achieve—the goal of complete formal specifications and programming-language implementations that are verifiably consistent with those specifications. Nevertheless, the joint history of these notations shows how supporting abstractions at one scale enables exploration of abstractions at a larger scale.

Abstractions in Software Systems

In the beginning—that is to say, in the 1950s—software designers expressed programs and data directly in the representation provided by the computer hardware or in somewhat more legible "assembly languages" that mapped directly to the hardware. This required great conceptual leaps from problem domain to machine primitives, which limited the sophistication of the results. The late 1950s saw the introduction of programming languages that allowed the programmer to describe computations through formulas that were compiled into the hardware representation. Similarly, the descriptions of information representation originally referred directly to hardware memory locations ("the flag field is bits 6 to 8 of the third word of the record"). Programming languages of the 1960s developed notations for describing information in somewhat more abstract terms than the machine representation, so that the programmer could refer directly to "flag" and have that reference translated automatically to whichever bits were appropriate. Not only are the more abstract languages easier to read and write, but they also provide a degree of decoupling between the program and the underlying hardware representation that simplifies modification of the program.

In 1967 Knuth[2] showed us how to think systematically about the concept of a data structure (such as a stack, queue, list, tree, graph, matrix, or set) in isolation from its representation and about the concept of an algorithm (such as search, sort, traversal, or matrix inversion) in isolation from the particular program that implements it. This separation liberated us to think independently about the *abstraction*—the algorithms and data descriptions that describe a result and its *implementation*—the specific program and data declarations that implement those ideas on a computer.

The next few years saw the development of many elegant and sophisticated algorithms with associated data representations. Sometimes the speed of the algorithm depended on a special trick of representation. Such was the case with in-place heapsort, a sorting algorithm that begins by regarding—abstracting—the values to be sorted as a one-dimensional unsorted array. As the heapsort algorithm runs, it rearranges the values in a particularly elegant way so that one end of the array can be abstracted as a progressively growing tree, and when the algorithm terminates, the entire array has become an abstract tree with the sorted values in a simple-to-extract order. In most actual programs that implemented heapsort, though, these abstractions were not described explicitly, so any programmer who changed the program had to depend on intuition and sketchy, often obsolete, prose documentation to determine the original programmer's intentions. Further, the program that implemented the algorithms had no special relation to the data structures. This situation was fraught with opportunities for confusion and for lapses of discipline, which led to undocumented (frequently unintended) dependencies on representation tricks. Unsurprisingly, program errors often occurred when another programmer subsequently changed the data representation. In response to this problem, in the 1970s a notion of "type" emerged to help document

---

[2]Donald Knuth, 1967, *The Art of Computer Programming*, Vol. 1, Addison-Wesley, Boston, Mass.

the intended uses of data. For example, we came to understand that referring to record fields abstractly—by a symbolic name rather than by absolute offset from the start of a data block—made programs easier to understand as well as to modify, and that this could often be done without making the program run slower.

At the same time, the intense interest in algorithms dragged representation along as a poor cousin. In the early 1970s, there was a growing sense that "getting the data structures right" was a key to good software design. Parnas[3] elaborated this idea, arguing that a focus on data structures should lead to organizing software modules around data structures rather than around collections of procedures. Further, he advanced the then-radical proposition that *not* all information about how data is represented should be shared, because programmers who used the data would rely on things that might subsequently change. Better, he said, to specify what a module would accomplish and allow privileged access to the details only for selected code whose definition was in the same module as the representation. The abstract description should provide all the information required to use the component, and the implementer of the component would only be obligated to keep the promises made in that description. He elaborated this idea as "information hiding." Parnas subsequently spent several years at the Naval Research Laboratory applying these ideas to the specification of the A7E avionics system, showing that the idea could scale up to practical real-world systems.

This was one of the precursors of object-oriented programming and the marketplace for independently developed components that can be used unchanged in larger systems, from components that invoke by procedure calls from a larger system through java applets that download into Web browsers and third-party filters for photo-processing programs. Computer scientists are still working out the consequences of using abstract descriptions to encapsulate details. Abstractions can, in some circumstances, be used in many software systems rather than custom-defined for a specific use. However, the interactions between parts can be subtle—including not only the syntactic rules for invoking the parts but also the semantics of their computations—and the problems associated with making independently developed parts work properly together remain an active research area.

So why isn't such a layered abstract description just a house of cards, ready to tumble down in the slightest whiff of wind? Because we partition our tasks so that we deal with different concerns at different levels of

---

[3]David L. Parnas, 1972, "On the Criteria to Be Used in Decomposing Systems into Modules," *Communications of the ACM* 15(2):1053-1058.

abstraction; by establishing reasonable confidence in each level of abstraction and understanding the relations between the levels, we build our confidence in the whole system. Some of our confidence is operational: we use tools with a demonstrated record of success. Chief among these tools are the programming languages, supported by compilers that automatically convert the abstractions to code (see Aho and Larus in this chapter). Other confidence comes from testing—a kind of end-to-end check that the actual software behaves, at least to the extent we can check, like the system we intended to develop. Deeper confidence is instilled by formal analysis of the symbolic representation of the software, which brings us to the second part of the story.

Specifications of Software Systems

In the beginning, programming was an art form and debugging was very much ad hoc. In 1967, Floyd[4] showed how to reason formally about the effect a program has on its data. More concretely, he showed that for each operation a simple program makes, you can state a formal relation between the previous and following program state; further, you can compose these relations to determine what the program actually computes. Specifically he showed that given a program, a claim about what that program computes, and a formal definition of the programming language, you can derive the starting conditions, if any, for which that claim is true. Hoare and Dijkstra created similar but different formal rules for reasoning about programs in Pascal-like languages in this way.

The immediate reaction, that programs could be "proved correct" (actually, that the implementation of a program could be shown to be consistent with its specification) proved overly optimistic. However, the possibility of reasoning formally about a program changed the way people thought about programming and stimulated interest in formal specification of components and of programming languages—for precision in explanation, if not for proof. Formal specifications have now been received well for making intentions precise and for some specific classes of analysis, but the original promise remains unfulfilled. For example, there remains a gap between specifications of practical real-world systems and the complete, static specifications of the dream. Other remaining problems include effective specifications of properties other than functionality, tractability of analysis, and scaling to problems of realistic size.

---

[4]R.W. Floyd, 1967, "Assigning Meanings to Programs," *Proceedings of Symposia in Applied Mathematics*, Vol. 19-32, American Mathematical Society, Providence, R.I.

In 1972, Hoare[5] showed how to extend this formalized reasoning to encapsulations of the sort Parnas was exploring. This showed how to formalize the crucial abstraction step that expresses the relation between the abstraction and its implementation. Later in the 1970s, theoretical computer scientists linked the pragmatic notion of types that allowed compilers to do some compile-time checking to a theoretical model of type theory.

One of the obstacles to "proving programs correct" was the difficulty in creating a correct formal definition of the programming language in which the programs were written. The first approach was to add formal specifications to the programming language, as in Alphard, leaving proof details to the programmer. The formal analysis task was daunting, and it was rarely carried out. Further, many of the properties of interest about a particular program do not lend themselves to expression in formal logic. The second approach was to work hard on a simple common programming language such as Pascal to obtain formal specifications of the language semantics with only modest changes to the language, with a result such as Euclid. This revealed capabilities of programming languages that do not lend themselves to formalization. The third approach was to design a family of programming languages such as ML that attempt to include only constructs that lend themselves to formal analysis (assuming, of course, a correct implementation of the compiler). These languages require a style of software development that is an awkward match for many software problems that involve explicit state and multiple cooperating threads of execution.

Formal specifications have found a home in practice not so much in verification of full programs as in the use of specifications to clarify requirements and design. The cost of repairing a problem increases drastically the later the problem is discovered, so this clarification is of substantial practical importance. In addition, specific critical aspects of a program may be analyzed formally, for example through static analysis or model checking.

The Interaction of Abstraction and Specification

This brings us to the third part of our story: the coupling between progress in the operational notations of programming languages and the descriptive notations of formal specification systems. We can measure

---

[5]C.A.R. Hoare, 1972, "Proofs of Correctness of Data Representations," *Acta Informatica* 1:271-281.

progress in programming language abstraction, at least qualitatively, by the scale of the supported abstractions—the quantity of machine code represented by a single abstract construct. We can measure progress in formal specification, equally qualitatively, by the fraction of a complex software system that is amenable to formal specification and analysis. And we see in the history of both, that formal reasoning about programs has grown hand in hand with the capability of the languages to express higher-level abstractions about the software. Neither advances very far without waiting for the other to catch up.

We can see this in the development of type systems. One of the earliest type systems was the Fortran variable naming convention: operations on variables whose names began with I, J, K, L, or M were compiled with fixed-point arithmetic, while operations on all other variables were compiled with floating-point arithmetic. This approach was primitive, but it provided immediate benefit to the programmer, namely correct machine code. A few years later, Algol 60 provided explicit syntax for distinguishing types, but this provided little benefit to the programmer beyond the fixed/floating point discrimination—and it was often ignored. Later languages that enforced type checking ran into programmer opposition to taking the time to write declarations, and the practice became acceptable only when it became clear that the type declarations enabled analysis that was immediately useful, namely discovering problems at compile time rather than execution time.

So type systems originally entered programming languages as a mechanism for making sure at compile time that the run-time values supplied for expression evaluation or procedure calls would be legitimate. (Morris later called this "Neanderthal verification.") But the nuances of this determination are subtle and extensive, and type systems soon found a role in the research area of formal semantics of programming languages. Here they found a theoretical constituency, spawning their own problems and solutions.

Meanwhile, abstract data types were merging with the inheritance mechanisms of Smalltalk to become object-oriented design and programming models. The inheritance mechanisms provided ways to express complex similarities among types, and the separation of specification from implementation in abstract data types allowed management of the code that implemented families of components related by inheritance. Inheritance structures can be complex, and formal analysis techniques for reasoning about these structures soon followed.

With wider adoption of ML-like languages in the 1990s, the functional programming languages began to address practical problems, thereby drawing increasing attention from software developers for whom correctness is a critical concern—and for whom the prospect of assurances about the software justifies extra investment in analysis.

The operational abstraction and symbolic analysis lines of research made strong contact again in the development of the Java language, which incorporates strong assurances about type safety with object-oriented abstraction.

So two facets of programming language design—language mechanisms to support abstraction and incorporation of formal specification and semantics in languages—have an intertwined history, with advances on each line stimulated by problems from both lines, and with progress on one line sometimes stalled until the other line catches up.

Additional Observations

How are the results of research on languages, models, and formalisms to be evaluated? For operational abstractions, the models and the detailed specifications of relevant properties have a utilitarian function, so appropriate evaluation criteria should reflect the needs of software developers. Expertise in any field requires not only higher-order reasoning skills, but also a large store of facts, together with a certain amount of context about their implications and appropriate use.[6] It follows that models and tools intended to support experts should support rich bodies of operational knowledge. Further, they should support large vocabularies of established knowledge as well as the theoretical base for deriving information of interest.

Contrast this with the criteria against which mathematical systems are evaluated. Mathematics values elegance and minimality of mechanism; derived results are favored over added content because they are correct and consistent by their construction. These criteria are appropriate for languages whose function is to help understand the semantic basis of programming languages and the possibility of formal reasoning.

Given the differences in appropriate base language size that arise from the different objectives, it is small wonder that different criteria are appropriate, or that observers applying such different criteria reach different conclusions about different research results.

---

[6]This is true across a wide range of problem domains; studies have demonstrated it for medical diagnosis, physics, chess, financial analysis, architecture, scientific research, policy decision making, and others (Raj Reddy, 1988, "Foundations and Grand Challenges of Artificial Intelligence," *AI Magazine*, Winter; Herbert A. Simon, 1989, "Human Experts and Knowledge-based Systems," pp. 1-21 in *Concepts and Characteristics of Knowledge-based Systems* (M. Tokoro, Y. Anzai, and A. Yonezawa, eds.), North-Holland Publishing, Amsterdam).

PROGRAMMING LANGUAGES AND COMPUTER SCIENCE

*Alfred V. Aho, Columbia University, and
James Larus, Microsoft Research*

Software affects virtually every modern person's life, often profoundly, but few appreciate the vast size and scope of the worldwide infrastructure behind it or the ongoing research aimed at improving it. Hundreds of billions of lines of software code are currently in use, with many more billions added annually, and they virtually run the gamut of conceivable applications. It has been possible to build all this software because we have been successful in inventing a wide spectrum of programming languages for describing the tasks we want computers to do. But like human languages, they are sometimes quirky and imperfect. Thus computer scientists are continually evolving more accurate, expressive, and convenient ways in which humans may communicate to computers.

Programming languages are different in many respects from human languages. A computer is capable of executing arithmetic or logical operations at blinding speeds, but it is in fact a device that's frustratingly simpleminded—forever fixed in a concrete world of bits, bytes, arithmetic, and logic (see Hill in Chapter 2). Thus a computer must be given straightforward, unambiguous, step-by-step instructions. Humans, by contrast, can often solve highly complex problems using their innate strengths of formulating and employing abstraction.

To get a feel for the extent of this "semantic gap," imagine explaining to a young child how to prepare a meal. Given that the child likely has no experience or context to draw upon, every step must be described clearly and completely, and omitting even the simplest detail can lead to a messy failure. Explaining tasks to computers is in many ways more difficult, because computers not only require far more detail but that detail must also be expressed in a primitive difficult-to-read notation such as binary numbers.

As an example of how programming languages bridge the gap between programmers and computers, consider numerical computation, one of the earliest applications of computers, dating back to World War II. A common mathematical operation is to multiply two vectors of numbers. Humans will use a notation such as A*B to indicate the multiplication (i.e., dot product) of vector A and vector B—knowing that this is shorthand for all of the individual steps actually needed to perform the multiplication. Computers, on the other hand, know nothing about vectors or the rules for multiplying them. They can only move numbers around; perform addition, multiplication, and other primitive mathematical operations on them; and make simple decisions. Expressed in terms of these primitive operations, a simple vector multiplication routine might require roughly 20 computer instructions, while a more sophisticated version, which improves performance by using techniques like instruction-level parallelism and caches (see Hill in Chapter 2), might require a few hundred instructions. Someone looking at this machine-language routine could easily be excused for not spotting the simple mathematical operation embodied in the complicated sequence of machine instructions.

A high-level programming language addresses this "semantic gap" between human and machine in several ways. It can provide operations specifically designed to help formulate and solve a particular type of problem. A programming language specifically intended for numeric computation might use the human-friendly, concise notation A*B. It saves programmers from repeatedly reimplementing (or mis-implementing) the same operations. A software tool called a "compiler" translates the higher-level program into instructions executable by a computer.

Programmers soon realized that a program written in a high-level language could be run on more than one computer. Because the hardware peculiarities of a particular computer could be hidden in a compiler, rather than exposed in a language, programs could often be written in a portable language that can be run on several computers. This separation of high-level programs and computers expanded the market for commercial software and helped foster the innovative software industry.

Another advantage of compilers is that a program written in a high-level language often runs faster. Compilers, as a result of several decades of fundamental research on program analysis, code generation, and code-optimization techniques, are generally far better at translating programs into efficient sequences of computer instructions than are human programmers. The comparison is interesting and edifying.

Programmers can occasionally produce small and ingenious pieces of machine code that run much faster than the machine instructions generated by a compiler. However, as a program grows to thousands of lines or more, a compiler's systematic, analytical approach usually results in higher-quality translations that not only execute far more effectively but also contain fewer errors.

Program optimization is a very fertile area of computer science research. A compiler improves a program by changing the process by which it computes its result to a slightly different approach that executes faster. A compiler is allowed to make a change only if it does not affect the result that the program computes.

Interestingly, true optimization is a goal that is provably impossible. An analysis algorithm that predicts if a nontrivial modification affects a program's result can be used to solve the program equivalence problem, which is provably impossible because of Turing's result (see Kleinberg and Papadimitriou in Chapter 2). Compilers side-step this conundrum by modifying a program only when it is possible to demonstrate that the change leaves the program's result unaffected. Otherwise, they assume the worst and leave alone programs in which there is any doubt about the consequences of a change. The interplay between Turing's fundamental result, which predates programming languages and compilers by many years, and the vast number of practical and effective tools for analyzing and optimizing programs is emblematic of computer science as a whole, which continues to make steady progress despite many fundamental limitations on computability.

The past half century has seen the development of thousands of programming languages that use many different approaches to writing programs. For example, some languages, so-called imperative languages, specify *how* a computation is to be done, while declarative languages focus on *what* the computer is supposed to do. Some languages are general-purpose, but many others are intended for specific application domains. For example, the languages C and C++ are commonly used in systems programming, SQL in writing queries for databases, and PostScript in describing the layout of printed material. Innovations and new applications typically produce new languages. For example, the Internet spurred development of Java for writing client/server applications and JavaScript and Flash for animating Web pages.

One might ask, "Are all of these languages necessary?" Turing's research on the nature of computing (see Kleinberg and Papadimitriou in Chapter 2) offers one answer to this question. Since almost every programming language is equivalent to Turing's universal computing machine, they are all in principle capable of expressing the same algorithms. But the choice of an inappropriate language can greatly complicate programming. It is not unlike asking whether a bicycle, car, and airplane are interchangeable modes of transportation. Just as it would be cumbersome, at best, to fly a jet to the grocery store to buy milk, so using the wrong programming language can make a program much longer and much more difficult to write and execute.

Today, most programs are written by teams of programmers. In this world, many programming problems and errors arise from misunderstandings of intent, misinformation, and human shortcomings, so language designers have come to recognize that programming languages convey information among human programmers, as well as to computers.

Language designers soon realized that programming languages must be extensible as well as computationally universal, as no one language could provide operations appropriate for all types of problems. Languages today offer many general mechanisms for programmers to use in addressing their specific problems. One of the early and most fundamental of these mechanisms introduced into programming languages was the "procedure," which collects and names the code to perform a particular operation. So, for example, a programmer who wants to implement operations that involve multiplying vectors in a language in which this capability is not built in could create a procedure with a meaningful name, such as "MultiplyVector," and simply cite that name to invoke that procedure whenever needed—as opposed to rewriting the same set of instructions each time. And programmers could then use the procedure in other programs rather than reinventing the wheel each time. Procedures of this sort have understandably become the fundamental building blocks of today's programs.

Another early insight is built on the fact that statements in a program typically execute in one of a small number of different patterns; thus the patterns themselves could be added to the vocabulary of a language rather than relying on a programmer to express the patterns with simpler (and a larger number of) statements. For example, a common idiom is to execute a group of statements repeatedly while a condition holds true. This is written:

```
while (condition) do
statements
```

Earlier languages did not provide this feature and instead relied on programmers to construct it, each time it was needed, from simpler statements:

```
test:
if (not condition) then goto done;
  statements
  goto test;
done:
```

The latter approach has several problems: the program is longer, the programmer's intent is more difficult to discern, and possibilities for errors increase. For example, if the first statement said "goto test" instead of "goto done," this piece of code would never terminate.

Incorporation of new constructs to aid in the development of more robust software systems has been a continuing major trend in programming-language development. In addition to well-structured features for controlling programs such as the "while loop," other improvements include features that permit dividing up software into modules, strong type checking to catch some errors at compile time rather than run time, and incorporation of automated memory management that frees the programmer from worrying about details of allocating and deallocating storage. These features not only improve the ability of a programming language to express a programmer's intent but also offer better facilities for detecting inconsistencies and other errors in programs.

Today's huge and ever-growing software infrastructure presents an enormous challenge for programmers, software companies, and society as whole. Because programs are written by people, they contain defects known as bugs. Even the best programs, written using the most advanced software engineering techniques, contain between 10 and 10,000 errors per million lines of new code. Some defects are minor, while others have the potential to disrupt society significantly.

The constantly evolving programming languages, techniques, and tools have done much to improve the quality of software. But the software revolution is always in need of some sweetening. Programming-language researchers are devoting increasing attention to producing programs with far fewer defects and systems with much higher levels of fault tolerance. They are also developing software verification tools of greater power and rigor that can be used throughout the software development process. The ultimate research goal is to produce programming languages and software development tools with which robust software systems can be created routinely and economically for all of tomorrow's applications.

5

Data, Representation, and Information

The preceding two chapters address the creation of models that capture phenomena of interest and the abstractions both for data and for computation that reduce these models to forms that can be executed by computer. We turn now to the ways computer scientists deal with information, especially in its static form as data that can be manipulated by programs.

Gray begins by narrating a long line of research on databases—storehouses of related, structured, and durable data. We see here that the objects of research are not data per se but rather designs of "schemas" that allow deliberate inquiry and manipulation. Gray couples this review with introspection about the ways in which database researchers approach these problems.

Databases support storage and retrieval of information by defining—in advance—a complex structure for the data that supports the intended operations. In contrast, Lesk reviews research on retrieving information from documents that are formatted to meet the needs of applications rather than predefined schematized formats.

Interpretation of information is at the heart of what historians do, and Ayers explains how information technology is transforming their paradigms. He proposes that history is essentially model building—constructing explanations based on available information—and suggests that the methods of computer science are influencing this core aspect of historical analysis.

DATABASE SYSTEMS:
A TEXTBOOK CASE OF RESEARCH PAYING OFF

Jim Gray, Microsoft Research

A small research investment helped produce U.S. market dominance in the $14 billion database industry. Government and industry funding of a few research projects created the ideas for several generations of products and trained the people who built those products. Continuing research is now creating the ideas and training the people for the next generation of products.

Industry Profile

The database industry generated about $14 billion in revenue in 2002 and is growing at 20 percent per year, even though the overall technology sector is almost static. Among software sectors, the database industry is second only to operating system software. Database industry leaders are all U.S.-based corporations: IBM, Microsoft, and Oracle are the three largest. There are several specialty vendors: Tandem sells over $1 billion/year of fault-tolerant transaction processing systems, Teradata sells about $1 billion/year of data-mining systems, and companies like Information Resources Associates, Verity, Fulcrum, and others sell specialized data and text-mining software.

In addition to these well-established companies, there is a vibrant group of small companies specializing in application-specific databases—for text retrieval, spatial and geographical data, scientific data, image data, and so on. An emerging group of companies offer XML-oriented databases. Desktop databases are another important market focused on extreme ease of use, small size, and disconnected (offline) operation.

Historical Perspective

Companies began automating their back-office bookkeeping in the 1960s. The COBOL programming language and its record-oriented file model were the workhorses of this effort. Typically, a batch of transactions was applied to the old-tape-master, producing a new-tape-master and printout for the next business day. During that era, there was considerable experimentation with systems to manage an online database that could capture transactions as they happened. At first these systems were ad hoc, but late in that decade network and hierarchical database products emerged. A COBOL subcommittee defined a network data model standard (DBTG) that formed the basis for most systems during the 1970s. Indeed, in 1980 DBTG-based Cullinet was the leading software company.

However, there were some problems with DBTG. DBTG uses a low-level, record-at-a-time procedural language to access information. The programmer has to navigate through the database, following pointers from record to record. If the database is redesigned, as often happens over a decade, then all the old programs have to be rewritten.

The relational data model, enunciated by IBM researcher Ted Codd in a 1970 *Communications of the Association for Computing Machinery* article,[1] was a major advance over DBTG. The relational model unified data and metadata so that there was only one form of data representation. It defined a non-procedural data access language based on algebra or logic. It was easier for end users to visualize and understand than the pointers-and-records-based DBTG model.

The research community (both industry and university) embraced the relational data model and extended it during the 1970s. Most significantly, researchers showed that a non-procedural language could be compiled to give performance comparable to the best record-oriented database systems. This research produced a generation of systems and people that formed the basis for products from IBM, Ingres, Oracle, Informix, Sybase, and others. The SQL relational database language was standardized by ANSI/ISO between 1982 and 1986. By 1990, virtually all database systems provided an SQL interface (including network, hierarchical, and object-oriented systems).

Meanwhile the database research agenda moved on to geographically distributed databases and to parallel data access. Theoretical work on distributed databases led to prototypes that in turn led to products. Today, all the major database systems offer the ability to distribute and replicate data among nodes of a computer network. Intense research on data replication during the late 1980s and early 1990s gave rise to a second generation of replication products that are now the mainstays of mobile computing.

Research of the 1980s showed how to execute each of the relational data operators in parallel—giving hundred-fold and thousand-fold speedups. The results of this research began to appear in the products of several major database companies. With the proliferation of data mining in the 1990s, huge databases emerged. Interactive access to these databases requires that the system use multiple processors and multiple disks to read all the data in parallel. In addition, these problems require near-

---

[1]E.F. Codd, 1970, "A Relational Model of Data from Large Shared Data Banks," *Communications of the ACM* 13(6):377-387. Available online at http://www.acm.org/classics/nov95/.

linear time search algorithms. University and industrial research of the previous decade had solved these problems and forms the basis of the current VLDB (very large database) data-mining systems.

Rollup and drilldown data reporting systems had been a mainstay of decision-support systems ever since the 1960s. In the middle 1990s, the research community really focused on data-mining algorithms. They invented very efficient data cube and materialized view algorithms that form the basis for the current generation of business intelligence products.

The most recent round of government-sponsored research creating a new industry comes from the National Science Foundation's Digital Libraries program, which spawned Google. It was founded by a group of "database" graduate students who took a fresh look at how information should be organized and presented in the Internet era.

Current Research Directions

There continues to be active and valuable research on representing and indexing data, adding inference to data search, compiling queries more efficiently, executing queries in parallel, integrating data from heterogeneous data sources, analyzing performance, and extending the transaction model to handle long transactions and workflow (transactions that involve human as well as computer steps). The availability of huge volumes of data on the Internet has prompted the study of data integration, mediation, and federation in which a portal system presents a unification of several data sources by pulling data on demand from different parts of the Internet.

In addition, there is great interest in unifying object-oriented concepts with the relational model. New data types (image, document, and drawing) are best viewed as the methods that implement them rather than by the bytes that represent them. By adding procedures to the database system, one gets active databases, data inference, and data encapsulation. This object-oriented approach is an area of active research and ferment both in academe and industry. It seems that in 2003, the research prototypes are mostly done and this is an area that is rapidly moving into products.

The Internet is full of semi-structured data—data that has a bit of schema and metadata, but is mostly a loose collection of facts. XML has emerged as the standard representation of semi-structured data, but there is no consensus on how such data should be stored, indexed, or searched. There have been intense research efforts to answer these questions. Prototypes have been built at universities and industrial research labs, and now products are in development.

The database research community now has a major focus on stream data processing. Traditionally, databases have been stored locally and are updated by transactions. Sensor networks, financial markets, telephone calls, credit card transactions, and other data sources present streams of data rather than a static database. The stream data processing researchers are exploring languages and algorithms for querying such streams and providing approximate answers.

Now that nearly all information is online, data security and data privacy are extremely serious and important problems. A small, but growing, part of the database community is looking at ways to protect people's privacy by limiting the ways data is used. This work also has implications for protecting intellectual property (e.g., digital rights management, watermarking) and protecting data integrity by digitally signing documents and then replicating them so that the documents cannot be altered or destroyed.

Case Histories

The U.S. government funded many database research projects from 1972 to the present. Projects at the University of California at Los Angeles gave rise to Teradata and produced many excellent students. Projects at Computer Corp. of America (SDD-1, Daplex, Multibase, and HiPAC) pioneered distributed database technology and object-oriented database technology. Projects at Stanford University fostered deductive database technology, data integration technology, query optimization technology, and the popular Yahoo! and Google Internet sites. Work at Carnegie Mellon University gave rise to general transaction models and ultimately to the Transarc Corporation. There have been many other successes from AT&T, the University of Texas at Austin, Brown and Harvard Universities, the University of Maryland, the University of Michigan, Massachusetts Institute of Technology, Princeton University, and the University of Toronto among others. It is not possible to enumerate all the contributions here, but we highlight three representative research projects that had a major impact on the industry.

Project INGRES

Project Ingres started at the University of California at Berkeley in 1972. Inspired by Codd's paper on relational databases, several faculty members (Stonebraker, Rowe, Wong, and others) started a project to design and build a relational system. Incidental to this work, they invented a query language (QUEL), relational optimization techniques, a language binding technique, and interesting storage strategies. They also pioneered work on distributed databases.

The Ingres academic system formed the basis for the Ingres product now owned by Computer Associates. Students trained on Ingres went on to start or staff all the major database companies (AT&T, Britton Lee, HP, Informix, IBM, Oracle, Tandem, Sybase). The Ingres project went on to investigate distributed databases, database inference, active databases, and extensible databases. It was rechristened Postgres, which is now the basis of the digital library and scientific database efforts within the University of California system. Recently, Postgres spun off to become the basis for a new object-relational system from the start-up Illustra Information Technologies.

System R

Codd's ideas were inspired by seeing the problems IBM and its customers were having with IBM's IMS product and the DBTG network data model. His relational model was at first very controversial; people thought that the model was too simplistic and that it could never give good performance. IBM Research management took a gamble and chartered a small (10-person) systems effort to prototype a relational system based on Codd's ideas. That system produced a prototype that eventually grew into the DB2 product series. Along the way, the IBM team pioneered ideas in query optimization, data independence (views), transactions (logging and locking), and security (the grant-revoke model). In addition, the SQL query language from System R was the basis for the ANSI/ISO standard.

The System R group went on to investigate distributed databases (project R*) and object-oriented extensible databases (project Starburst). These research projects have pioneered new ideas and algorithms. The results appear in IBM's database products and those of other vendors.

Gamma

Not all research ideas work out. During the 1970s there was great enthusiasm for database machines—special-purpose computers that would be much faster than general-purpose operating systems running conventional database systems. These research projects were often based on exotic hardware like bubble memories, head-per-track disks, or associative RAM. The problem was that general-purpose systems were improving at 50 percent per year, so it was difficult for exotic systems to compete with them. By 1980, most researchers realized the futility of special-purpose approaches and the database-machine community switched to research on using arrays of general-purpose processors and disks to process data in parallel.

The University of Wisconsin hosted the major proponents of this idea in the United States. Funded by the government and industry, those researchers prototyped and built a parallel database machine called

Gamma. That system produced ideas and a generation of students who went on to staff all the database vendors. Today the parallel systems from IBM, Tandem, Oracle, Informix, Sybase, and Microsoft all have a direct lineage from the Wisconsin research on parallel database systems. The use of parallel database systems for data mining is the fastest-growing component of the database server industry.

The Gamma project evolved into the Exodus project at Wisconsin (focusing on an extensible object-oriented database). Exodus has now evolved to the Paradise system, which combines object-oriented and parallel database techniques to represent, store, and quickly process huge Earth-observing satellite databases.

And Then There Is Science

In addition to creating a huge industry, database theory, science, and engineering constitute a key part of computer science today. Representing knowledge within a computer is one of the central challenges of computer science (Box 5.1). Database research has focused primarily on this fundamental issue. Many universities have faculty investigating these problems and offer classes that teach the concepts developed by this research program.

BOX 5.1
How Do You Know? A Long-Range View of Database Research

How can knowledge be represented so that algorithms can make new inferences from the knowledge base? This problem has challenged philosophers for millennia. There has been progress. Euclid axiomized geometry and proved its basic theorems, and in doing so implicitly demonstrated mechanical reasoning from first principles. George Boole's Laws of Thought created a predicate calculus, and Laplace's work on probability was a first start on statistical inference.

Each of these threads—proofs, predicate calculus, and statistical inference—were major advances; but each requires substantial human creativity to fit new problems to the solution. Wouldn't it be nice if we could just put all the books and journals in a library that would automatically organize them and start producing new answers?

There are huge gaps between our current tools and the goal of a self-organizing library, but computer scientists are trying to fill the gaps with better algorithms and better ways of representing knowledge. Databases are one branch of this effort to represent information and reason about it. The database community has taken a bottom-up approach, working with simple data representations and developing a calculus for asking and answering questions about the database.

continued

BOX 5.1 Continued

The fundamental approach of database researchers is to insist that the information must be schematized—the information must be represented in a predefined schema that assigns a meaning to each value. The author-title-subject-abstract schema of a library system is a typical example of this approach. The schema is used both to organize the data and to make it easy to express questions about the database.

Database researchers have labored to make it easy to define the schema, easy to add data to the database, and easy to pose questions to the database. Early database systems were dreadfully difficult to use—largely because we lacked the algorithms to automatically index huge databases and lacked powerful query tools. Today there are good tools to define schemas, and graphical tools that make it easy to explore and analyze the contents of a database.

This has required invention at all levels of the problem. At the lowest levels we had to discover efficient algorithms to sort, index, and organize numeric, text, temporal, and spatial information so that higher-level software could just pick from a wide variety of organizations and algorithms. These low-level algorithms mask data placement so that it can be spread among hundreds or thousands of disks; they mask concurrency so that the higher-level software can view a consistent data snapshot, even though the data is in flux. The low-level software includes enough redundancy so that once data is placed in the database, it is safe to assume that the data will never be lost. One major advance was the theory and algorithms to automatically guarantee these concurrency-reliability properties.

Text, spatial, and temporal databases have always posed special challenges. Certainly there have been huge advances in indexing these databases, but researchers still have many more problems to solve. The advent of image, video, and sound databases raises new issues. In particular, we are now able to extract a huge number of features from images and sounds, but we have no really good ways to index these features. This is just another aspect of the "curse of dimensionality" faced by database systems in the data-mining and data analysis area. When each object has more than a dozen attributes, traditional indexing techniques give little help in reducing the approximate search space.

So, there are still many unsolved research challenges for the low-level database "plumbers."

The higher-level software that uses this plumbing has been a huge success. Early on, the research community embraced the relational data model championed by Ted Codd. Codd advocated the use of non-procedural set-oriented programming to define schemas and to pose queries. After a decade of experimentation, these research ideas evolved into the SQL database language. Having this high-level non-procedural language was a boon both to application programmers and to database implementers. Application programmers could write much simpler programs. The database implementers faced the challenge of optimizing and executing SQL. Because it is so high level (SQL is a non-procedural functional dataflow language), SQL allows data to be distributed across many computers and disks. Because the programs do not mention any physical structures, the implementer is free to use whatever "plumbing" is available. And because the language is functional, it can be executed in parallel.

Techniques for implementing the relational data model and algorithms for efficiently executing database queries remain a core part of the database research agenda. Over the last decade, the traditional database systems have grown to include analytics (data cubes), and also data-mining algorithms borrowed from the machine-learning and statistics communities. There is increasing interest in solving information retrieval and multimedia database issues.

Today, there are very good tools for defining and querying traditional database systems; but, there are still major research challenges in the traditional database field. The major focus is automating as much of the data administration tasks as possible—making the database system self-healing and self-managing.

We are still far from the goal of building systems that automatically ingest information, reason about it, and produce answers on demand. But the goal is closer, and it seems attainable within this century.

COMPUTER SCIENCE IS TO INFORMATION AS CHEMISTRY IS TO MATTER

Michael Lesk, Rutgers University

In other countries computer science is often called "informatics" or some similar name. Much computer science research derives from the need to access, process, store, or otherwise exploit some resource of useful information. Just as chemistry is driven to large extent by the need to understand substances, computing is driven by a need to handle data and information. As an example of the way chemistry has developed, see Oliver Sacks's book *Uncle Tungsten: Memories of a Chemical Boyhood* (Vintage Books, 2002). He describes his explorations through the different metals, learning the properties of each, and understanding their applications. Similarly, in the history of computer science, our information needs and our information capabilities have driven parts of the research agenda. Information retrieval systems take some kind of information, such as text documents or pictures, and try to retrieve topics or concepts based on words or shapes. Deducing the concept from the bytes can be difficult, and the way we approach the problem depends on what kind of bytes we have and how many of them we have.

Our experimental method is to see if we can build a system that will provide some useful access to information or service. If it works, those algorithms and that kind of data become a new field: look at areas like geographic information systems. If not, people may abandon the area until we see a new motivation to exploit that kind of data. For example, face-recognition algorithms have received a new impetus from security needs, speeding up progress in the last few years. An effective strategy to move computer science forward is to provide some new kind of information and see if we can make it useful.

Chemistry, of course, involves a dichotomy between substances and reactions. Just as we can (and frequently do) think of computer science in terms of algorithms, we can talk about chemistry in terms of reactions. However, chemistry has historically focused on substances: the encyclopedias and indexes in chemistry tend to be organized and focused on compounds, with reaction names and schemes getting less space on the shelf. Chemistry is becoming more balanced as we understand reactions better; computer science has always been more heavily oriented toward algorithms, but we cannot ignore the driving force of new kinds of data.

The history of information retrieval, for example, has been driven by the kinds of information we could store and use. In the 1960s, for example, storage was extremely expensive. Research projects were limited to text materials. Even then, storage costs meant that a research project could just barely manage to have a single ASCII document available for processing. For example, Gerard Salton's SMART system, one of the leading text retrieval systems for many years (see Salton's book, *The SMART Automatic Retrieval System*, Prentice-Hall, 1971), did most of its processing on collections of a few hundred abstracts. The only collections of "full documents" were a collection of 80 extended abstracts, each a page or two long, and a collection of under a thousand stories from *Time Magazine*, each less than a page in length. The biggest collection was 1400 abstracts in aeronautical engineering. With this data, Salton was able to experiment on the effectiveness of retrieval methods using suffixing, thesauri, and simple phrase finding. Salton also laid down the standard methodology for evaluating retrieval systems, based on Cyril Cleverdon's measures of "recall" (percentage of the relevant material that is retrieved in response to a query) and "precision" (the percentage of the material retrieved that is relevant). A system with perfect recall finds all relevant material, making no errors of omission and leaving out nothing the user wanted. In contrast, a system with perfect precision finds only relevant material, making no errors of commission and not bothering the user with stuff of no interest. The SMART system produced these measures for many retrieval experiments and its methodology was widely used, making text retrieval one of the earliest areas of computer science with agreed-on evaluation methods. Salton was not able to do anything with image retrieval at the time; there were no such data available for him.

Another idea shaped by the amount of information available was "relevance feedback," the idea of identifying useful documents from a first retrieval pass in order to improve the results of a later retrieval. With so few documents, high precision seemed like an unnecessary goal. It was simply not possible to retrieve more material than somebody could look at. Thus, the research focused on high recall (also stimulated by the insistence by some users that they had to have every single relevant document). Relevance feedback helped recall. By contrast, the use of phrase searching to improve precision was tried but never got much attention simply because it did not have the scope to produce much improvement in the running systems.

The basic problem is that we wish to search for concepts, and what we have in natural language are words and phrases. When our documents are few and short, the main problem is not to miss any, and the research at the time stressed algorithms that found related words via associations or improved recall with techniques like relevance feedback.

Then, of course, several other advances—computer typesetting and word processing to generate material and cheap disks to hold it—led to much larger text collections. Figure 5.1 shows the decline in the price of

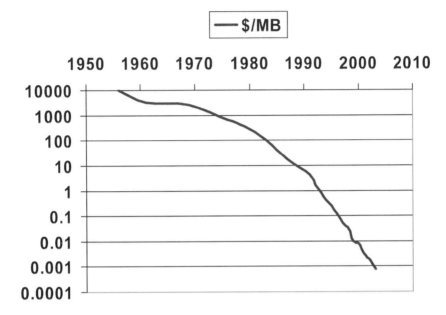

FIGURE 5.1 Decline in the price of disk space, 1950 to 2004.

disk space since the first disks in the mid-1950s, generally following the cost-performance trends of Moore's law.

Cheaper storage led to larger and larger text collections online. Now there are many terabytes of data on the Web. These vastly larger volumes mean that precision has now become more important, since a common problem is to wade through vastly too many documents. Not surprisingly, in the mid-1980s efforts started on separating the multiple meanings of words like "bank" or "pine" and became the research area of "sense disambiguation."[2] With sense disambiguation, it is possible to imagine searching for only one meaning of an ambiguous word, thus avoiding many erroneous retrievals.

Large-scale research on text processing took off with the availability of the TREC (Text Retrieval Evaluation Conference) data. Thanks to the National Institute of Standards and Technology, several hundred megabytes of text were provided (in each of several years) for research use. This stimulated more work on query analysis, text handling, searching

---

[2]See Michael Lesk, 1986, "How to Tell a Pine Cone from an Ice Cream Cone," *Proceedings SIGDOC*, pp. 26-28.

algorithms, and related areas; see the series titled *TREC Conference Proceedings*, edited by Donna Harmon of NIST.

Document clustering appeared as an important way to shorten long search results. Clustering enables a system to report not, say, 5000 documents but rather 10 groups of 500 documents each, and the user can then explore the group or groups that seem relevant. Salton anticipated the future possibility of such algorithms, as did others.[3] Until we got large collections, though, clustering did not find application in the document retrieval world. Now one routinely sees search engines using these techniques, and faster clustering algorithms have been developed.

Thus the algorithms explored switched from recall aids to precision aids as the quantity of available data increased. Manual thesauri, for example, have dropped out of favor for retrieval, partly because of their cost but also because their goal is to increase recall, which is not today's problem. In terms of finding the concepts hinted at by words and phrases, our goals now are to sharpen rather than broaden these concepts: thus disambiguation and phrase matching, and not as much work on thesauri and term associations.

Again, multilingual searching started to matter, because multilingual collections became available. Multilingual research shows a more precise example of particular information resources driving research. The Canadian government made its Parliamentary proceedings (called *Hansard*) available in both French and English, with paragraph-by-paragraph translation. This data stimulated a number of projects looking at how to handle bilingual material, including work on automatic alignment of the parallel texts, automatic linking of similar words in the two languages, and so on.[4]

A similar effect was seen with the Brown corpus of tagged English text, where the part of speech of each word (e.g., whether a word is a noun or a verb) was identified. This produced a few years of work on algorithms that learned how to assign parts of speech to words in running text based on statistical techniques, such as the work by Garside.[5]

---

[3]See, for example, N. Jardine and C.J. van Rijsbergen, 1971, "The Use of Hierarchical Clustering in Information Retrieval," *Information Storage and Retrieval* 7:217-240.

[4]See, for example, T.K. Landauer and M.L. Littman, 1990, "Fully Automatic Cross-Language Document Retrieval Using Latent Semantic Indexing," *Proceedings of the Sixth Annual Conference of the UW Centre for the New Oxford English Dictionary and Text Research,* pp. 31-38, University of Waterloo Centre for the New OED and Text Research, Waterloo, Ontario, October; or I. Dagan and Ken Church, 1997, "Termight: Coordinating Humans and Machines in Bilingual Terminology Acquisition," *Machine Translation* 12(1/2):89-107.

[5]Roger Garside, 1987, "The CLAWS Word-tagging System," in R. Garside, G. Leech, and G. Sampson (eds.), *The Computational Analysis of English: A Corpus-Based Approach*, Longman, London.

One might see an analogy to various new fields of chemistry. The recognition that pesticides like DDT were environmental pollutants led to a new interest in biodegradability, and the Freon propellants used in aerosol cans stimulated research in reactions in the upper atmosphere. New substances stimulated a need to study reactions that previously had not been a top priority for chemistry and chemical engineering.

As storage became cheaper, image storage was now as practical as text storage had been a decade earlier. Starting in the 1980s we saw the IBM QBIC project demonstrating that something could be done to retrieve images directly, without having to index them by text words first.[6] Projects like this were stimulated by the availability of "clip art" such as the COREL image disks. Several different projects were driven by the easy access to images in this way, with technology moving on from color and texture to more accurate shape processing. At Berkeley, for example, the "Blobworld" project made major improvements in shape detection and recognition, as described in Carson et al.[7] These projects demonstrated that retrieval could be done with images as well as with words, and that properties of images could be found that were usable as concepts for searching.

Another new kind of data that became feasible to process was sound, in particular human speech. Here it was the Defense Advanced Research Projects Agency (DARPA) that took the lead, providing the SWITCH-BOARD corpus of spoken English. Again, the availability of a substantial file of tagged information helped stimulate many research projects that used this corpus and developed much of the technology that eventually went into the commercial speech recognition products we now have. As with the TREC contests, the competitions run by DARPA based on its spoken language data pushed the industry and the researchers to new advances. National needs created a new technology; one is reminded of the development of synthetic rubber during World War II or the advances in catalysis needed to make explosives during World War I.

Yet another kind of new data was geo-coded data, introducing a new set of conceptual ideas related to place. Geographical data started showing up in machine-readable form during the 1980s, especially with the release of the Dual Independent Map Encoding (DIME) files after the 1980

---

[6]See, for example, Wayne Niblack, Ron Barber, William Equitz, Myron Flickner, Eduardo H. Glasman, Dragutin Petkovic, Peter Yanker, Christos Faloutsos, and Gabriel Taubin, 1993, "The QBIC Project: Querying Images by Content, Using Color, Texture, and Shape," *Storage and Retrieval for Image and Video Databases (SPIE)*, pp. 173-187.

[7]C. Carson, M. Thomas, S. Belongie, J.M. Hellerstein, and J. Malik, 1999, "Blobworld: A System for Region-based Image Indexing and Retrieval," *Proceedings of the Third Annual Conference on Visual Information Systems*, Springer-Verlag, Amsterdam, pp. 509-516.

census and the Topologically Integrated Geographic Encoding and Referencing (TIGER) files from the 1990 census. The availability, free of charge, of a complete U.S. street map stimulated much research on systems to display maps, to give driving directions, and the like.[8] When aerial photographs also became available, there was the triumph of Microsoft's "Terraserver," which made it possible to look at a wide swath of the world from the sky along with correlated street and topographic maps.[9]

More recently, in the 1990s, we have started to look at video search and retrieval. After all, if a CD-ROM contains about 300,000 times as many bytes per pound as a deck of punched cards, and a digitized video has about 500,000 times as many bytes per second as the ASCII script it comes from, we should be about where we were in the 1960s with video today. And indeed there are a few projects, most notably the Informedia project at Carnegie Mellon University, that experiment with video signals; they do not yet have ways of searching enormous collections, but they are developing algorithms that exploit whatever they can find in the video: scene breaks, closed-captioning, and so on.

Again, there is the problem of deducing concepts from a new kind of information. We started with the problem of words in one language needing to be combined when synonymous, picked apart when ambiguous, and moved on to detecting synonyms across multiple languages and then to concepts depicted in pictures and sounds. Now we see research such as that by Jezekiel Ben-Arie associating words like "run" or "hop" with video images of people doing those actions. In the same way we get again new chemistry when molecules like "buckyballs" are created and stimulate new theoretical and reaction studies.

Defining concepts for search can be extremely difficult. For example, despite our abilities to parse and define every item in a computer language, we have made no progress on retrieval of software; people looking for search or sort routines depend on metadata or comments. Some areas seem more flexible than others: text and naturalistic photograph processing software tends to be very general, while software to handle CAD diagrams and maps tends to be more specific. Algorithms are sometimes portable; both speech processing and image processing need Fourier transforms, but the literature is less connected than one might like (partly

---

[8]An early publication was R. Elliott and M. Lesk, 1982, "Route Finding in Street Maps by Computers and People," *Proceedings of the AIII-82 National Conference on Artificial Intelligence*, Pittsburgh, Pa., August, pp. 258-261.

[9]T. Barclay, J. Gray, and D. Slutz, 2000, "Microsoft Terraserver: A Spatial Data Warehouse," *Proceedings of ACM SIGMOD*, Association for Computing Machinery, New York, pp. 307-318.

because of the difference between one-dimensional and two-dimensional transforms).

There are many other examples of interesting computer science research stimulated by the availability of particular kinds of information. Work on string matching today is often driven by the need to align sequences in either protein or DNA data banks. Work on image analysis is heavily influenced by the need to deal with medical radiographs. And there are many other interesting projects specifically linked to an individual data source. Among examples:

• The British Library scanning of the original manuscript of *Beowulf* in collaboration with the University of Kentucky, working on image enhancement until the result of the scanning is better than reading the original;

• The Perseus project, demonstrating the educational applications possible because of the earlier Thesaurus Linguae Graecae project, which digitized all the classical Greek authors;

• The work in astronomical analysis stimulated by the Sloan Digital Sky Survey;

• The creation of the field of "forensic paleontology" at the University of Texas as a result of doing MRI scans of fossil bones;

• And, of course, the enormous amount of work on search engines stimulated by the Web.

When one of these fields takes off, and we find wide usage of some online resource, it benefits society. Every university library gained readers as their catalogs went online and became accessible to students in their dorm rooms. Third World researchers can now access large amounts of technical content their libraries could rarely acquire in the past.

In computer science, and in chemistry, there is a tension between the algorithm/reaction and the data/substance. For example, should one look up an answer or compute it? Once upon a time logarithms were looked up in tables; today we also compute them on demand. Melting points and other physical properties of chemical substances are looked up in tables; perhaps with enough quantum mechanical calculation we could predict them, but it's impractical for most materials. Predicting tomorrow's weather might seem a difficult choice. One approach is to measure the current conditions, take some equations that model the atmosphere, and calculate forward a day. Another is to measure the current conditions, look in a big database for the previous day most similar to today, and then take the day after that one as the best prediction for tomorrow. However, so far the meteorologists feel that calculation is better. Another complicated example is chess: given the time pressure of chess tournaments against speed and storage available in computers, chess programs do the opening and the endgame by looking in tables of old data and calculate for the middle game.

To conclude, a recipe for stimulating advances in computer science is to make some data available and let people experiment with it. With the incredibly cheap disks and scanners available today, this should be easier than ever. Unfortunately, what we gain with technology we are losing to law and economics. Many large databases are protected by copyright; few motion pictures, for example, are old enough to have gone out of copyright. Content owners generally refuse to grant permission for wide use of their material, whether out of greed or fear: they may have figured out how to get rich off their files of information or they may be afraid that somebody else might have. Similarly it is hard to get permission to digitize in-copyright books, no matter how long they have been out of print. Jim Gray once said to me, "May all your problems be technical." In the 1960s I was paying people to key in aeronautical abstracts. It never occurred to us that we should be asking permission of the journals involved (I think what we did would qualify as fair use, but we didn't even think about it). Today I could scan such things much more easily, but I would not be able to get permission. Am I better off or worse off?

There are now some 22 million chemical substances in the Chemical Abstracts Service Registry and 7 million reactions. New substances continue to intrigue chemists and cause research on new reactions, with of course enormous interest in biochemistry both for medicine and agriculture. Similarly, we keep adding data to the Web, and new kinds of information (photographs of dolphins, biological flora, and countless other things) can push computer scientists to new algorithms. In both cases, synthesis of specific instances into concepts is a crucial problem. As we see more and more kinds of data, we learn more about how to extract meaning from it, and how to present it, and we develop a need for new algorithms to implement this knowledge. As the data gets bigger, we learn more about optimization. As it gets more complex, we learn more about representation. And as it gets more useful, we learn more about visualization and interfaces, and we provide better service to society.

HISTORY AND THE FUNDAMENTALS OF COMPUTER SCIENCE

Edward L. Ayers, University of Virginia

We might begin with a thought experiment: What is history? Many people, I've discovered, think of it as books and the things in books. That's certainly the explicit form in which we usually confront history. Others, thinking less literally, might think of history as stories about the past; that would open us to oral history, family lore, movies, novels, and the other forms in which we get most of our history.

All these images are wrong, of course, in the same way that images of atoms as little solar systems are wrong, or pictures of evolution as profiles of ever taller and more upright apes and people are wrong. They are all models, radically simplified, that allow us to think about such things in the exceedingly small amounts of time that we allot to these topics.

The same is true for history, which is easiest to envision as technological progress, say, or westward expansion, of the emergence of freedom— or of increasing alienation, exploitation of the environment, or the growth of intrusive government.

Those of us who think about specific aspects of society or nature for a living, of course, are never satisfied with the stories that suit the purposes of everyone else so well.

We are troubled by all the things that don't fit, all the anomalies, variance, and loose ends. We demand more complex measurement, description, and fewer smoothing metaphors and lowest common denominators.

Thus, to scientists, atoms appear as clouds of probability; evolution appears as a branching, labyrinthine bush in which some branches die out and others diversify. It can certainly be argued that past human experience is as complex as anything in nature and likely much more so, if by complexity we mean numbers of components, variability of possibilities, and unpredictability of outcomes.

Yet our means of conveying that complexity remain distinctly analog: the story, the metaphor, the generalization. Stories can be wonderfully complex, of course, but they are complex in specific ways: of implication, suggestion, evocation. That's what people love and what they remember.

But maybe there is a different way of thinking about the past: as information. In fact, information is *all* we have. Studying the past is like studying scientific processes for which you have the data but cannot run the experiment again, in which there is no control, and in which you can never see the actual process you are describing and analyzing. All we have is information in various forms: words in great abundance, billions of numbers, millions of images, some sounds and buildings, artifacts.

The historian's goal, it seems to me, should be to account for as much of the complexity embedded in that information as we can. That, it appears, is what scientists do, and it has served them well.

And how has science accounted for ever-increasing amounts of complexity in the information they use? Through ever more sophisticated instruments. The connection between computer science and history could be analogous to that between telescopes and stars, microscopes and cells. We could be on the cusp of a new understanding of the patterns of complexity in human behavior of the past.

The problem may be that there is too much complexity in that past, or too much static, or too much silence. In the sciences, we've learned how to filter, infer, use indirect evidence, and fill in the gaps, but we have a much more literal approach to the human past.

We have turned to computer science for tasks of more elaborate description, classification, representation. The digital archive my colleagues and I have built, the Valley of the Shadow Project, permits the manipulation of millions of discrete pieces of evidence about two communities in the era of the American Civil War. It uses sorting mechanisms, hypertextual display, animation, and the like to allow people to handle the evidence of this part of the past for themselves. This isn't cutting-edge computer science, of course, but it's darned hard and deeply disconcerting to some, for it seems to abdicate responsibility, to undermine authority, to subvert narrative, to challenge story.

Now, we're trying to take this work to the next stage, to analysis. We have composed a journal article that employs an array of technologies, especially geographic information systems and statistical analysis in the creation of the evidence. The article presents its argument, evidence, and historiographical context as a complex textual, tabular, and graphical representation. XML offers a powerful means to structure text and XSL an even more powerful means to transform it and manipulate its presentation. The text is divided into sections called "statements," each supported with "explanation." Each explanation, in turn, is supported by evidence and connected to relevant historiography.

Linkages, forward and backward, between evidence and narrative are central. The historiography can be automatically sorted by author, date, or title; the evidence can be arranged by date, topic, or type. Both evidence and historiographical entries are linked to the places in the analysis where they are invoked. The article is meant to be used online, but it can be printed in a fixed format with all the limitations and advantages of print.

So, what are the implications of thinking of the past in the hard-headed sense of admitting that all we really have of the past is information? One implication might be great humility, since all we have for most of the past are the fossils of former human experience, words frozen in ink and images frozen in line and color. Another implication might be hubris: if we suddenly have powerful new instruments, might we be on the threshold of a revolution in our understanding of the past? We've been there before.

A connection between history and social science was tried before, during the first days of accessible computers. Historians taught themselves statistical methods and even programming languages so that they could adopt the techniques, models, and insights of sociology and political science. In the 1950s and 1960s the creators of the new political history called on historians to emulate the precision, explicitness, replicability, and inclusivity of the quantitative social sciences. For two decades that quantitative history flourished, promising to revolutionize the field. And to a considerable extent it did: it changed our ideas of social mobility, political identification, family formation, patterns of crime, economic growth, and the consequences of ethnic identity. It explicitly linked the past to the present and held out a history of obvious and immediate use.

But that quantitative social science history collapsed suddenly, the victim of its own inflated claims, limited method and machinery, and changing academic fashion. By the mid-1980s, history, along with many of the humanities and social sciences, had taken the linguistic turn. Rather than software manuals and codebooks, graduate students carried books of French philosophy and German literary interpretation. The social science of choice shifted from sociology to anthropology; texts replaced tables. A new generation defined itself in opposition to social scientific methods just as energetically as an earlier generation had seen in those methods the best means of writing a truly democratic history. The first computer revolution largely failed.

The first effort at that history fell into decline in part because historians could not abide the distance between their most deeply held beliefs and what the statistical machinery permitted, the abstraction it imposed. History has traditionally been built around contingency and particularity, but the most powerful tools of statistics are built on sampling and extrapolation, on generalization and tendency. Older forms of social history talked about vague and sometimes dubious classifications in part because that was what the older technology of tabulation permitted us to see. It has become increasingly clear across the social sciences that such flat ways of describing social life are inadequate; satisfying explanations must be dynamic, interactive, reflexive, and subtle, refusing to reify structures of social life or culture. The new technology permits a new cross-fertilization.

Ironically, social science history faded just as computers became widely available, just as new kinds of social science history became feasible. No longer is there any need for white-coated attendants at huge mainframes and expensive proprietary software. Rather than reducing people to rows and columns, searchable databases now permit researchers to maintain the identities of individuals in those databases and to represent entire populations rather than samples. Moreover, the record can now include things social science history could only imagine before the Web: completely indexed newspapers, with the original readable on the screen; completely searchable letters and diaries by the thousands; and interactive maps with all property holders identified and linked to other records. Visualization of patterns in the data, moreover, far outstrips the possibilities of numerical calculation alone. Manipulable histograms, maps, and time lines promise a social history that is simultaneously sophisticated and accessible. We have what earlier generations of social science historians dreamed of: a fast and widely accessible network linked to cheap and powerful computers running common software with well-established standards for the handling of numbers, texts, and images. New possibilities of collaboration and cumulative research beckon. Perhaps the time is right to reclaim a worthy vision of a disciplined and explicit social scientific history that we abandoned too soon.

What does this have to do with computer science? Everything, it seems to me. If you want hard problems, historians have them. And what's the hardest problem of all right now? The capture of the very information that *is* history. Can computer science imagine ways to capture historical information more efficiently? Can it offer ways to work with the spotty, broken, dirty, contradictory, nonstandardized information we work with?

The second hard problem is the integration of this disparate evidence in time and space, offering new precision, clarity, and verifiability, as well as opening new questions and new ways of answering them.

If we can think of these ways, then we face virtually limitless possibilities. Is there a more fundamental challenge or opportunity for computer science than helping us to figure out human society over human time?

6

Achieving Intelligence

One of the great aspirations of computer science has been to understand and emulate capabilities that we recognize as expressive of intelligence in humans. Research has addressed tasks ranging from our sensory interactions with the world (vision, speech, locomotion) to the cognitive (analysis, game playing, problem solving). This quest to understand human intelligence in all its forms also stimulates research whose results propagate back into the rest of computer science—for example, lists, search, and machine learning.

Going beyond simply retrieving information, machine learning draws inferences from available data. Mitchell describes the application of classifying text documents automatically and shows how this research exemplifies the experiment-analyze-generalize style of experimental research.

One of the exemplars of intelligent behavior is natural-language processing in all its forms—including speech recognition and generation, natural-language understanding, and machine translation. Lee describes how, in the area of statistical natural-language understanding, the commitment to an empirical computational perspective draws meaning from data and brings interdisciplinary contributions together.

Games have frequently provided settings for exploring new computing techniques. They make excellent testbeds because they are usually circumscribed in scope, have well-defined rules, employ human-performance standards for comparison, and are not on the critical path to make-or-break projects. In addition, they are engaging and appealing, which makes it easy to recruit early users. Koller and Biermann examine the history of computer science endeavors in chess and checkers, showing how success depends both on "smarts" (improved representations and algorithms) and sheer computer power.

THE EXPERIMENT-ANALYZE-GENERALIZE LOOP IN COMPUTER SCIENCE RESEARCH: A CASE STUDY

Tom Mitchell, Carnegie Mellon University

Much research in computer science involves an iterative process of attacking some new application problem, developing a computer program to solve that specific problem, and then stepping back to learn a general principle or algorithm, along with a precise description of the general class of problems to which it can be applied. This experiment-analyze-generalize loop lies at the heart of experimental computer science research, and it is largely responsible for the continuous growth over several decades in our knowledge of robust, effective computer algorithms. Here we illustrate the approach with a case study involving machine-learning algorithms for automatically classifying text. In particular, we see how attempts to train a text classifier for classifying Web pages led to a fundamental insight into a new class of learning algorithms.

Automatically classifying text documents such as e-mails, Web pages, and online memos is a problem of obvious importance. It would clearly be useful for computers to automatically classify e-mails into categories such as "spam," "meeting invitations," and so on, or to automatically classify Web pages into categories such as "personal home page," "product announcement," and others. Computer scientists have studied the problem of automatic text classification for a number of years, over time developing increasingly effective algorithms that achieve higher classification accuracy and accommodate a broader range of text documents.

Machine Learning for Text Classification

One approach to developing text classification software involves machine learning. In most software development, programmers write detailed algorithms as line-by-line recipes to be executed by the computer. In contrast, machine learning involves training the software by instead showing it examples of inputs and outputs of the desired program. The computer then learns (estimates) the general input-output function from the examples provided. For instance, to train a program to classify Web pages into categories such as "personal home page" or "product description," we would present a set of training examples consisting of individual Web pages (example inputs) and the correct classification for each (example outputs). The machine-learning system uses these training examples to produce a general program that achieves high accuracy on these examples, and presumably on novel future inputs as well. While it is unrealistic to expect perfect classification accuracy over novel future examples, in fact these accuracies for many text classification problems are well above 90 percent, and are often higher than those that can be achieved by manual programming (because humans generally don't know the general classification rule either!).

What kind of machine-learning approach can analyze such training examples to learn the correct classification rule? One popular machine learning approach is a Bayesian classifier employing a bag-of-words representation for Web pages. The bag-of-words representation, depicted in Figure 6.1, describes each text document by the frequency of occurrence of each word in the document. Although this representation removes information such as the exact sequence in which words occur, it has been found to be highly effective for document classification.

Once the training-example Web pages are described in terms of their word frequencies, the classifier can calculate from these training examples the average frequency for each word, within each different class of Web pages. A new document can then be automatically classified by first observing its own word frequencies and then assigning it to the class whose average frequencies are most similar to its own. The naive Bayes classifier uses this general approach. More precisely, it uses the training data to estimate the probability $P(w_i | c_j)$ that a word drawn at random from a random document from class c_j will be the word w_i (e.g., $P(\text{"phone"} | \text{home page})$ is the probability that a random word found on a random home page will be the word "phone"). Thousands of such probability terms are estimated during training (i.e., if English contains approximately 10^5 words, and if we consider only two distinct classes of Web pages, then the program will estimate such 2×10^5 probabilities). These learned probabilities, along with the estimated class priors, are then used to classify a new document, d, by calculating the probability $P(w_i | d)$ that d belongs to the class c_j based on its observed words. Figure 6.2 summarizes the training and classification procedures for the naive Bayes classifier (this type of Bayes classifier is called "naïve" because it makes the assumption that words occur independently within documents of each class, and "Bayesian" because it uses Bayes rules along with the learned probability terms to classify new documents).

Improving Accuracy by Learning from Unlabeled Examples

Although the naive Bayes classifier can often achieve accuracies of 90 percent or higher when trained to discriminate classes of Web pages such as "personal home page" versus "academic course Web page," it often requires many hundreds or thousands of training examples to reach this accuracy. Thus, the primary cost in developing the classifier involves

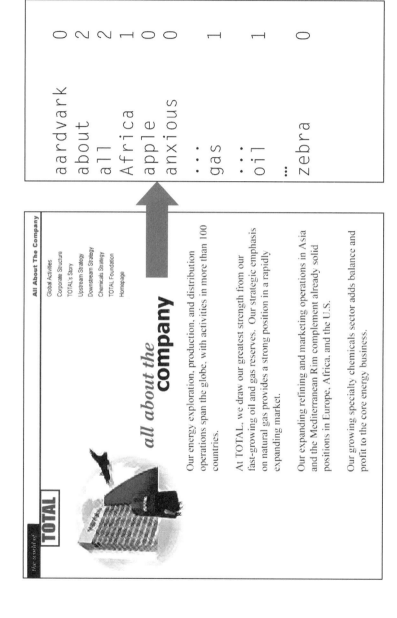

FIGURE 6.1 In the bag-of-words approach, text documents are described solely by the frequencies of the words they contain. Here, the Web page on the left is represented by the frequencies of each word it contains (shown by the list of words and frequencies on the right).

Train:

    For each class c_j of documents
    1. Estimate $P(c_j)$
    2. For each word w_i estimate $P(w_i \mid c_j)$

Classify (doc):

    Assign *doc* to most probable*class

$$\arg\max_{j} P(c_j) \prod_{w_i \in doc} P(w_i \mid c_j)$$

* assuming words are conditionally independent, given the class

FIGURE 6.2 Naïve Bayes Learner based on the bag-of-words representation from Figure 6.1.

hand-labeling the training examples. This leads to the interesting question: Can we devise learning methods that achieve higher accuracy when given unlabeled examples (e.g., additional Web pages without their classification) in addition to a set of labeled examples? At first it may seem that the answer must be no, because providing unlabeled examples amounts to providing an example input to the program without providing the desired output. Surprisingly, if the text documents we wish to classify are Web pages, then we shall see that the answer is yes, due to a particular characteristic of Web pages.

The characteristic that makes it possible to benefit from unlabeled data when learning to classify Web pages is illustrated in Figure 6.3. Note first that Web pages typically appear on the Web along with hyperlinks that point to them. We can therefore think of each example Web page as being described by two sets of features: the words occurring within the page (which we will call X_1) and the words occurring on hyperlinks that point to this page (which we will call X_2). Furthermore, in many cases the X_1 features alone are sufficient to classify the page without X_2 (i.e., even

Professor Faloutsos   My advisor

U.S. mail address:
Christos Faloutsos
Dept. of Computer Science
Carnegie Mellon University
Wean Hall
5000 Forbes Avenue
Pittsburgh, PA 15213-3891
Phone: (412)-268.14.57
Fax: (412)-268.55.76
Email: christos AT cs DOT cmu DOT edu

Christos Faloutsos

Current Position: Professor.
Courtesy appointment: Electrical and Computer Engineering, CMU (1998-2001)
Academic Degrees: Ph.D. and M.Sc. (University of Toronto.); B.Sc. (Nat. Tech. U. Athens)
Short bio
Weekly schedule

Related groups/projects:

- Database group at CMU
- Member of the Informedia project
- Member of CALD (Center for Automated Learning and Discovery)
- Member of PDL (Parallel Data Lab)
- co-PI for the Astrostatistics KDI-NSF project

FIGURE 6.3 Redundantly sufficient features for classifying Web pages. Note that the class of this Web page ("faculty home page") can be inferred from either (a) the words on the Web page or (b) the words on the hyperlinks that point to the page. In such cases we say that these two feature sets are "redundantly sufficient" to classify the example.

when ignoring the hyperlinks, it is obvious that the Web page of Figure 6.3 belongs to the class "faculty home page"). Similarly, the X_2 features taken alone may also be sufficient to classify the page (i.e., if the hyperlink pointing to the page contains the words "Professor Faloutsos," the page is most probably a "faculty home page"). In short, we say in this case that the features describing the example Web pages are *redundantly sufficient* to perform the classification. Furthermore, notice that the hyperlink words tend to be quite independent of the exact words on the page, given the class of the page (in part because the hyperlinks and the pages to which they point are often written by different authors).

This characteristic of Web pages suggests the following training procedure for using a combination of labeled and unlabeled examples: First, we use the labeled training examples to train two different naive Bayes classifiers. One of these classifiers uses only the X_1 features; the other uses only the X_2 features. The first classifier is then applied to the unlabeled training examples, and it selects the example d that it is most confident in classifying (i.e., the example that yields the highest probability $P(c_j | d)$). It is then allowed to assign that label to this previously unlabeled example, and the second classifier is now retrained using this new labeled example along with the original labeled examples. The identical process can be executed reversing the roles of the two classifiers, using each to train the other. This process is called co-training. Furthermore, the process can be repeated many times, each time assigning a few most-confident labels to the initially unlabeled examples.

Does this learning algorithm work in practice? It does. Blum and Mitchell,[1] for example, describe experiments using co-training to classify Web pages into the categories "academic course home page" or not. Starting with just 12 labeled Web pages, they found that co-training with an additional 788 unlabeled Web pages reduced the classification error rate by a factor of two, from 11 percent to 5 percent.

Analyze the Specific Solution to Generalize the Principle

Given the empirical success of this co-training algorithm for classifying Web pages, it is natural to ask: What is the general class of machine-learning problems for which unlabeled data can be proven to improve classification accuracy? Intuitively, the reason co-training works when learning to classify Web pages is that (1) the examples can be described by two different sets of features (hyperlink words, page words) that are redundantly sufficient, and (2) the two features are distributed somewhat independently, so that an example with an easy-to-classify hyperlink is likely to point to a Web page of average classification difficulty. We can

---

[1]A. Blum and T. Mitchell, 1998, "Combining Labeled and Unlabeled Data with Co-Training," *Proceedings of the 1998 Conference on Computational Learning Theory*, Association for Computing Machinery, New York.

therefore train two classifiers, using each to produce new, high-confidence labels for training the other.

Blum and Mitchell make this intuitive characterization more precise and formal.[2] They prove that for the class of learning problems they define, one can learn successfully from a small set of labeled examples and a larger volume of unlabeled examples. The essence of their characterization is as follows. In general, one can view the problem of learning a classifier as the problem of estimating some unknown classifier function $f: X \rightarrow Y$ given only a set of labeled input-output examples $\{\langle x_i, f(x_i)\rangle\}$ and a set of unlabeled examples $\{x_i\}$ with unknown output. The co-training problem setting can then be defined as a special case of learning a classifier, where (1) the input instances X can be described as $X_1 \times X_2$ (i.e., X_1 = hyperlink words, X_2 = Web page words), and where (2) one can compute f based on either X_1 or X_2 (formally, there exist functions g_1 and g_2 such that $f(x) = g_1(x_1) = g_2(x_2)$ for any $x = \langle x_1, x_2 \rangle$. They then go on to characterize the impact of unlabeled data on learning behavior in several situations. For example, they show that if one makes the additional assumption that X_1 and X_2 are conditionally independent given the class Y, then any function that is learnable from noisy labeled data can also be learned from a small set of labeled data that produces better-than-random accuracy, plus unlabeled data.

Summary

This case study shows how the attempt to find more accurate learning algorithms for Web page classification motivated the development of a specialized algorithm, which in turn motivated a formal analysis to understand the precise class of problems for which the learning algorithm could be proven to succeed. In fact, the insights provided by this analysis have, in turn, led to the development of more accurate learning algorithms for this class of problems (e.g., Collins and Singer,[3] and Muslea et al.[4]). Further-

---

[2] A. Blum and T. Mitchell, 1998, "Combining Labeled and Unlabeled Data with Co-Training," *Proceedings of the 1998 Conference on Computational Learning Theory*, Association for Computing Machinery, New York.

[3] M. Collins and Y. Singer, 1999, "Unsupervised Models for Named Entity Classification," *Proceedings of the Joint SIGDAT Conference on Empirical Methods in Natural Language Processing and Very Large Corpora*, Association for Computational Linguistics, East Stroudsburg, Pa., pp. 100-110.

[4] I. Muslea, S. Minton, and C. Knoblock, 2000, "Selective Sampling with Redundant Views," *Proceedings of the Seventeenth National Conference on Artificial Intelligence*, AAAI Press, Menlo Park, Calif., pp. 621-626.

more, it made it apparent that the co-training algorithm published by Blum and Mitchell was in fact similar to an earlier algorithm by Yarowski[5] for learning to disambiguate word senses (e.g., learning whether "bank" refers to a financial institution, or a place near a river). In Yarowski's case, the features X_1 and X_2 are the linguistic context in which the word occurs, and the document in which it occurs.

This case study illustrates the useful interplay between experiment and theory in advancing computer science. The advance in our understanding of the science of computation can be described in this case using statements of the form "for problems that exhibit structure S, algorithm A will exhibit property P." In some cases we have only experimental evidence to support conjectures of this form, in some cases analytical proofs, but in many cases a blend of the two, and a family of related statements rather than a single one.

Of course the interplay between experiment and analysis is generally messy, and not quite as clean as post facto reports would like to make it appear! In many cases the formal models motivated by specific applications do not fully capture the complexities of the application. In our own case study, for instance, the assumption that hyperlink words can be used to classify the Web page they point to is not quite valid—some hyperlink words such as "click here" provide no information at all about the page they point to! Nevertheless, theoretical characterizations of the problem are useful even if incomplete and approximate, provided they capture a significant problem structure that impacts on the design and performance of algorithms. And the experiment-analyze-generalize cycle of research often leads to a second and third generation of experiments and of theoretical models that better characterize the application problems, just as current theoretical research on using unlabeled data is now considering problem formalizations that relax the assumption violated by the "click here" hyperlinks.

---

[5]D. Yarowsky, 1995, "Unsupervised Word Sense Disambiguation Rivaling Supervised Methods," *Proceedings of the 33rd Annual Meeting of the Association for Computational Linguistics,* Association for Computational Linguistics, East Stroudsburg, Pa., pp. 189-196.

"I'M SORRY DAVE, I'M AFRAID I CAN'T DO THAT": LINGUISTICS, STATISTICS, AND NATURAL-LANGUAGE PROCESSING CIRCA 2001

Lillian Lee, Cornell University

> *It's the year 2000, but where are the flying cars? I was promised flying cars.*
> —Avery Brooks, IBM commercial

According to many pop-culture visions of the future, technology will eventually produce the Machine That Can Speak to Us. Examples range from the False Maria in Fritz Lang's 1926 film *Metropolis* to Knight Rider's KITT (a talking car) to *Star Wars'* C-3PO (said to have been modeled on the False Maria). And, of course, there is the HAL 9000 computer from *2001: A Space Odyssey*; in one of the film's most famous scenes, the astronaut Dave asks HAL to open a pod bay door on the spacecraft, to which HAL responds, "I'm sorry Dave, I'm afraid I can't do that."

Natural-language processing, or NLP, is the field of computer science devoted to creating such machines—that is, enabling computers to use human languages both as input and as output. The area is quite broad, encompassing problems ranging from simultaneous multi-language translation to advanced search engine development to the design of computer interfaces capable of combining speech, diagrams, and other modalities simultaneously. A natural consequence of this wide range of inquiry is the integration of ideas from computer science with work from many other fields, including linguistics, which provides models of language; psychology, which provides models of cognitive processes; information theory, which provides models of communication; and mathematics and statistics, which provide tools for analyzing and acquiring such models.

The interaction of these ideas together with advances in machine learning (see Mitchell in this chapter) has resulted in concerted research activity in statistical natural-language processing: making computers language-enabled by having them acquire linguistic information directly from samples of language itself. In this essay, we describe the history of statistical NLP; the twists and turns of the story serve to highlight the sometimes complex interplay between computer science and other fields.

Although currently a major focus of research, the data-driven, computational approach to language processing was for some time held in deep disregard because it directly conflicts with another commonly held viewpoint: human language is so complex that language samples alone seemingly cannot yield enough information to understand it. Indeed, it is often said that NLP is "AI-complete" (a pun on NP-completeness; see

Kleinberg and Papadimitriou in Chapter 2), meaning that the most difficult problems in artificial intelligence manifest themselves in human language phenomena. This belief in language use as the touchstone of intelligent behavior dates back at least to the 1950 proposal of the Turing Test[6] as a way to gauge whether machine intelligence has been achieved; as Turing wrote, "The question and answer method seems to be suitable for introducing almost any one of the fields of human endeavor that we wish to include."

The reader might be somewhat surprised to hear that language understanding is so hard. After all, human children get the hang of it in a few years, word processing software now corrects (some of) our grammatical errors, and TV ads show us phones capable of effortless translation. One might therefore be led to believe that HAL is just around the corner.

Such is not the case, however. In order to appreciate this point, we temporarily divert from describing statistical NLP's history—which touches upon Hamilton versus Madison, the sleeping habits of colorless green ideas, and what happens when one fires a linguist—to examine a few examples illustrating why understanding human language is such a difficult problem.

Ambiguity and Language Analysis

At last, a computer that understands you like your mother.
                                                    —1985 McDonnell-Douglas ad

The snippet quoted above indicates the early confidence at least one company had in the feasibility of getting computers to understand human language. But in fact, that very sentence is illustrative of the host of difficulties that arise in trying to analyze human utterances, and so, ironically, it is quite unlikely that the system being promoted would have been up to the task. A moment's reflection reveals that the sentence admits at least three different interpretations:

1. The computer understands you as well as your mother understands you.
2. The computer understands that you like your mother.
3. The computer understands you as well as it understands your mother.

---

[6]Roughly speaking, a computer will have passed the Turing Test if it can engage in conversations indistinguishable from those of a human.

That is, the sentence is ambiguous; and yet we humans seem to instantaneously rule out all the alternatives except the first (and presumably the intended) one. We do so based on a great deal of background knowledge, including understanding what advertisements typically try to convince us of. How are we to get such information into a computer?

A number of other types of ambiguity are also lurking here. For example, consider the speech recognition problem: how can we distinguish between this utterance, when spoken, and ". . . a computer that understands your lie cured mother"? We also have a word sense ambiguity problem: how do we know that here "mother" means "a female parent," rather than the Oxford English Dictionary-approved alternative of "a cask or vat used in vinegar-making"? Again, it is our broad knowledge about the world and the context of the remark that allows us humans to make these decisions easily.

Now, one might be tempted to think that all these ambiguities arise because our example sentence is highly unusual (although the ad writers probably did not set out to craft a strange sentence). Or, one might argue that these ambiguities are somehow artificial because the alternative interpretations are so unrealistic that an NLP system could easily filter them out. But ambiguities crop up in many situations. For example, in "Copy the local patient files to disk" (which seems like a perfectly plausible command to issue to a computer), is it the patients or the files that are local?[7] Again, we need to know the specifics of the situation in order to decide. And in multilingual settings, extra ambiguities may arise. Here is a sequence of seven Japanese *kanji* characters:

$$社長兼業務部長$$

Since Japanese doesn't have spaces between words, one is faced with the initial task of deciding what the component words are. In particular, this character sequence corresponds to at least two possible word sequences, "president, both, business, general-manager" (= "a president as well as a general manager of business") and "president, subsidiary-business, Tsutomu (a name), general-manager" (= ?). It requires a fair bit of linguistic information to choose the correct alternative.[8]

---

[7]Or, perhaps, the files themselves are patient? But our knowledge about the world rules this possibility out.

[8]To take an analogous example in English, consider the non-word-delimited sequence of letters "theyouthevent." This corresponds to the word sequences "the youth event," "they out he vent," and "the you the vent."

To sum up, we see that the NLP task is highly daunting, for to resolve the many ambiguities that arise in trying to analyze even a single sentence requires deep knowledge not just about language but also about the world. And so when HAL says, "I'm afraid I can't do that," NLP researchers are tempted to respond, "I'm afraid you might be right."

Firth Things First

But before we assume that the only viable approach to NLP is a massive knowledge-engineering project, let us go back to the early approaches to the problem. In the 1940s and 1950s, one prominent trend in linguistics was explicitly empirical and in particular distributional, as exemplified by the work of Zellig Harris (who started the first linguistics program in the United States). The idea was that correlations (co-occurrences) found in language data are important sources of information, or, as the influential linguist J.R. Firth declared in 1957, "You shall know a word by the company it keeps."

Such notions accord quite happily with ideas put forth by Claude Shannon in his landmark 1948 paper establishing the field of information theory; speaking from an engineering perspective, he identified the probability of a message's being chosen from among several alternatives, rather than the message's actual content, as its critical characteristic. Influenced by this work, Warren Weaver in 1949 proposed treating the problem of translating between languages as an application of cryptography (see Sudan in Chapter 7), with one language viewed as an encrypted form of another. And Alan Turing's work on cracking German codes during World War II led to the development of the Good-Turing formula, an important tool for computing certain statistical properties of language.

In yet a third area, 1941 saw the statisticians Frederick Mosteller and Frederick Williams address the question of whether it was Alexander Hamilton or James Madison who wrote the various pseudonymous *Federalist Papers*. Unlike previous attempts, which were based on historical data and arguments, Mosteller and Williams used the patterns of word occurrences in the texts as evidence. This work led up to the famed Mosteller and Wallace statistical study that many consider to have settled the authorship of the disputed papers.

Thus, we see arising independently from a variety of fields the idea that language can be viewed from a data-driven, empirical perspective—and a data-driven perspective leads naturally to a computational perspective.

A "C" Change

However, data-driven approaches fell out of favor in the late 1950s. One of the commonly cited factors is a 1957 argument by linguist (and student of Harris) Noam Chomsky, who believed that language behavior should be analyzed at a much deeper level than its surface statistics. He claimed,

> It is fair to assume that neither sentence (1) [Colorless green ideas sleep furiously] nor (2) [Furiously sleep ideas green colorless] . . . has ever occurred. . . . Hence, in any [computed] statistical model . . . these sentences will be ruled out on identical grounds as equally "remote" from English. Yet (1), though nonsensical, is grammatical, while (2) is not.[9]

That is, we humans know that sentence (1), which at least obeys (some) rules of grammar, is indeed more probable than (2), which is just word salad; but (the claim goes), since both sentences are so rare, they will have identical statistics—i.e., a frequency of zero—in any sample of English. Chomsky's criticism is essentially that data-driven approaches will always suffer from a lack of data, and hence are doomed to failure.

This observation turned out to be remarkably prescient: even now, when billions of words of text are available online, perfectly reasonable phrases are not present. Thus, the so-called sparse data problem continues to be a serious challenge for statistical NLP even today. And so, the effect of Chomsky's claim, together with some negative results for machine learning and a general lack of computing power at the time, was to cause researchers to turn away from empirical approaches and toward knowledge-based approaches where human experts encoded relevant information in computer-usable form.

This change in perspective led to several new lines of fundamental, interdisciplinary research. For example, Chomsky's work viewing language as a formal, mathematically describable object has had a lasting impact on both linguistics and computer science; indeed, the Chomsky hierarchy, a sequence of increasingly more powerful classes of grammars, is a staple of the undergraduate computer science curriculum. Conversely, the highly influential work of, among others, Kazimierz Adjukiewicz, Joachim Lambek, David K. Lewis, and Richard Montague adopted the lambda calculus, a fundamental concept in the study of programming languages, to model the semantics of natural languages.

---

[9]Interestingly, this claim has become so famous as to be self-negating, as simple Web searches on "Colorless green ideas sleep furiously" and its reversal will show.

The Empiricists Strike Back

By the 1980s, the tide had begun to shift once again, in part because of the work done by the speech recognition group at IBM. These researchers, influenced by ideas from information theory, explored the power of probabilistic models of language combined with access to much more sophisticated algorithmic and data resources than had previously been available. In the realm of speech recognition, their ideas form the core of the design of modern systems; and given the recent successes of such software—large-vocabulary continuous-speech recognition programs are now available on the market—it behooves us to examine how these systems work.

Given some acoustic signal, which we denote by the variable a, we can think of the speech recognition problem as that of transcription: determining what sentence is most likely to have produced a. Probabilities arise because of the ever-present problem of ambiguity: as mentioned above, several word sequences, such as "your lie cured mother" versus "you like your mother," can give rise to similar spoken output. Therefore, modern speech recognition systems incorporate information both about the acoustic signal and the language behind the signal. More specifically, they rephrase the problem as determining which sentence s maximizes the product $P(a \mid s) \times P(s)$. The first term measures how likely the acoustic signal would be if s were actually the sentence being uttered (again, we use probabilities because humans don't pronounce words the same way all the time). The second term measures the probability of the sentence s itself; for example, as Chomsky noted, "colorless green ideas sleep furiously" is intuitively more likely to be uttered than the reversal of the phrase. It is in computing this second term, $P(s)$, where statistical NLP techniques come into play, since accurate estimation of these sentence probabilities requires developing probabilistic models of language. These models are acquired by processing tens of millions of words or more. This is by no means a simple procedure; even linguistically naive models require the use of sophisticated computational and statistical techniques because of the sparse data problem foreseen by Chomsky. But using probabilistic models, large datasets, and powerful learning algorithms (both for $P(s)$ and $P(a \mid s)$) has led to our achieving the milestone of commercial-grade speech recognition products capable of handling continuous speech ranging over a large vocabulary.

But let us return to our story. Buoyed by the successes in speech recognition in the 1970s and 1980s (substantial performance gains over knowledge-based systems were posted), researchers began applying data-driven approaches to many problems in natural-language processing, in a turn-around so extreme that it has been deemed a "revolution." Indeed, now empirical methods are used at all levels of language analysis. This is not just due to increased resources: a succession of breakthroughs in machine-learning algorithms has allowed us to leverage existing resources much more effectively. At the same time, evidence from psychology shows that human learning may be more statistically based than previously thought; for instance, work by Jenny Saffran, Richard Aslin, and Elissa Newport reveals that 8-month-old infants can learn to divide continuous speech into word segments based simply on the statistics of sounds following one another. Hence, it seems that the "revolution" is here to stay.

Of course, we must not go overboard and mistakenly conclude that the successes of statistical NLP render linguistics irrelevant (rash statements to this effect have been made in the past, e.g., the notorious remark, "every time I fire a linguist, my performance goes up"). The information and insight that linguists, psychologists, and others have gathered about language is invaluable in creating high-performance broad-domain language understanding systems; for instance, in the speech recognition setting described above, a better understanding of language structure can lead to better language models. Moreover, truly interdisciplinary research has furthered our understanding of the human language faculty. One important example of this is the development of the head-driven phrase structure grammar (HPSG) formalism—this is a way of analyzing natural language utterances that truly marries deep linguistic information with computer science mechanisms, such as unification and recursive datatypes, for representing and propagating this information throughout the utterance's structure. In sum, although many challenges remain (for instance, while the speech-recognition systems mentioned above are very good at transcription, they are a long way from engaging in true language understanding), computational techniques and data-driven methods are now an integral part both of building systems capable of handling language in a domain-independent, flexible, and graceful way, and of improving our understanding of language itself.

Acknowledgments

Thanks to the members of and reviewers for the CSTB fundamentals of computer science study, and especially Alan Biermann, for their helpful feedback. Also, thanks to Alex Acero, Takako Aikawa, Mike Bailey, Regina Barzilay, Eric Brill, Chris Brockett, Claire Cardie, Joshua Goodman, Ed Hovy, Rebecca Hwa, John Lafferty, Bob Moore, Greg Morrisett, Fernando Pereira, Hisami Suzuki, and many others for stimulating discussions and very useful comments. Rie Kubota Ando provided the Japanese example. The use of the term "revolution" to describe the re-ascendance of statistical methods comes from Julia Hirschberg's 1998 invited address to the American Association for Artificial Intelligence. The McDonnell-Douglas ad and some of its analyses were presented in a lecture by Stuart Shieber. All errors are mine alone. This paper is based on work supported in part by the National Science Foundation under ITR/IM grant IIS-0081334 and a Sloan Research Fellowship. Any opinions, findings, and conclusions or recommendations expressed above are those of the author and do not necessarily reflect the views of the National Science Foundation or the Sloan Foundation.

Bibliography

Chomsky, Noam, 1957, "Syntactic Structures," Number IV in *Janua Linguarum.* Mouton, The Hague, The Netherlands.

Firth, John Rupert, 1957, "A Synopsis of Linguistic Theory 1930-1955," pp. 1-32 in the Philological Society's *Studies in Linguistic Analysis.* Blackwell, Oxford. Reprinted in *Selected Papers of J.R. Firth*, F. Palmer (ed.), Longman, 1968.

Good, Irving J., 1953, "The Population Frequencies of Species and the Estimation of Population Parameters," *Biometrika* 40(3,4):237-264.

Harris, Zellig, 1951, *Methods in Structural Linguistics*, University of Chicago Press. Reprinted by Phoenix Books in 1960 under the title *Structural Linguistics.*

Montague, Richard, 1974, *Formal Philosophy: Selected Papers of Richard Montague*, Richmond H. Thomason (ed.), Yale University Press, New Haven, Conn.

Mosteller, Frederick, and David L. Wallace, 1984, *Applied Bayesian and Classical Inference: The Case of the Federalist Papers*, Springer-Verlag. First edition published in 1964 under the title *Inference and Disputed Authorship: The Federalist.*

Pollard, Carl, and Ivan Sag, 1994, *Head-driven Phrase Structure Grammar*, University of Chicago Press and CSLI Publications.

Saffran, Jenny R., Richard N. Aslin, and Elissa L. Newport, 1996, "Statistical Learning by 8-Month-Old Infants," *Science* 274(5294):1926-1928, December.

Shannon, Claude E., 1948, "A Mathematical Theory of Communication," *Bell System Technical Journal* 27:379-423 and 623-656.

Turing, Alan M., 1950, "Computing Machinery and Intelligence," *Mind* LIX:433-460.

Weaver, Warren, 1949, "Translation," Memorandum. Reprinted in W.N. Locke and A.D. Booth, eds., *Machine Translation of Languages: Fourteen Essays*, MIT Press, Cambridge, Mass., 1955.

For Further Reading

Charniak, Eugene, 1993, *Statistical Language Learning*, MIT Press, Cambridge, Mass.

Jurafsky, Daniel, and James H. Martin, 2000, *Speech and Language Processing: An Introduction to Natural Language Processing, Computational Linguistics, and Speech Recognition*, Prentice Hall. Contributing writers: Andrew Keller, Keith Vander Linden, and Nigel Ward.

Manning, Christopher D., and Hinrich Schütze, 1999, *Foundations of Statistical Natural Language Processing*, MIT Press, Cambridge, Mass.

COMPUTER GAME PLAYING:
BEATING HUMANITY AT ITS OWN GAME

Daphne Koller, Stanford University, and
Alan Biermann, Duke University

The idea of getting a computer to play a complex game such as checkers or chess has been present in computer science research from its earliest days. The earliest effort even predated real computers. In 1769, Baron Wolfgang von Kempelen displayed a chess-playing automaton called "Turk." It drew a lot of attention, until people realized that the cabinet of the "machine" concealed a human dwarf who was a chess expert.

The first real attempt to show how a computer could play a game was by Claude Shannon, one of the fathers of information science. The basic idea is to define a game tree that tells us all of the possible move sequences in the game. We can then ask, at each point in the tree, what a rational (selfish) player would do at that point. The answer comes from an analysis of the game tree beginning at the end of the tree (the termination of the game). For example, assume that one player has black pieces and the other white pieces. We can mark each game termination point as B—black wins, W—white wins, or D—draw. Then we can work our way from the termination points of the game backwards: If the white player, at her turn, has a move leading to a position marked W, then she can take that move and guarantee a win; in this case, this position is labeled with W. Otherwise, if she has a move leading to a position marked D, then she can force a draw, and the position is labeled with D. If all of her moves lead to positions marked B, then this position is a guaranteed win for black (assuming he plays optimally), and it is marked with B. Similar propagation rules apply to positions controlled by the black player. Thus, assuming perfect play by each player, we can completely understand the win potential of every board position.

This procedure is a great theoretical tool for thinking about a game. For example, it shows that, assuming both players play perfectly, we can determine without playing a single move which of the players will win, or if the game has a forced draw. We simply carry out the above procedure and check whether the initial position is marked with a B, a W, or a D. Unfortunately, for almost all realistic games, this procedure cannot be carried out because the size of the computation is too large. For example, the game tree for chess has approximately 10^{120} trajectories. As Shannon points out, a computer that evaluated a million positions per second would require over 10^{95} years just to decide on its first move!

Shannon's idea was to explore only part of the game tree. At each position, the computer looks forward a certain number of steps, and then somehow evaluates the positions reached even if they are not wins or losses. For example, it can give a higher score to positions where it has more pieces. The computer then selects an optimal move relative to that myopic perspective about the game.

Turing, the inventor of the Turing machine (see "Computability and Complexity" by Kleinberg and Papadimitriou in Chapter 2) was the first to try and implement this idea. He wrote the first program capable of playing a full game of chess. But this program never ran on a computer; it was hand-simulated against a very weak player, who managed to beat it anyway.

The first attempt to get an actual computer to play a full-scale real game was made by Arthur Samuel. In the mid-1940s, Samuel was a professor of electrical engineering at the University of Illinois and became active in a project to design one of the first electronic computers. It was there that he conceived the idea of a checkers program that would beat the world champion and demonstrate the power of electronic computers. Apparently the program was not finished while he was at the University of Illinois, perhaps because the computer was not completed in time.

In 1949, Samuel joined IBM's Poughkeepsie Laboratory and worked on IBM's first stored program computer, the 701. Samuel's work on checkers was not part of his job. He did the work in his spare time, without telling his supervisors. He got the computer operators (who had to authorize and run all computer programs) to run his program by telling them it was testing the capabilities of the 701. This program was one of the first programs to run on IBM's very first production computer. The computer spent its days being tested for accounting and scientific computation, and its nights playing checkers.

Interestingly, Samuel's justification for using the machine was actually valid. Indeed, because his checkers program was one of the earliest examples of non-numerical computation, Samuel greatly influenced the instruction set of early IBM computers. The logical instructions of these computers were put in at his instigation and were quickly adopted by all computer designers, because they are useful for most non-numerical computation.

Samuel's program was the first to play checkers at a reasonable level. It not only implemented Shannon's ideas; it also extended them substantially by introducing new and important algorithmic ideas. For example, Shannon's original proposal was to search all of the paths in the game up to a given depth. Samuel's program used a more sophisticated algorithm, called alpha-beta pruning, that avoided exploring paths that it could prove were suboptimal. This algorithm allowed Samuel to almost double the number of steps that it looked into the future before making the decision.

Alpha-beta pruning allowed Samuel's program to prune large numbers of paths in the tree that would never be taken in optimal play. Consider the example in Figure 6.4. Here, the machine, playing white, has two moves, leading to positions A and B. The machine examines the paths that continue beyond position A and determines that the quality (according to some measure) of the best position it can reach from A is 10. It then starts evaluating position B, where the black player moves. The first move by black leads to position B1; this position is evaluated, by exploring the paths below it, to have a value of 5 (to white). Now, consider any other move by black, say to B2. Either B2 is worth more than 5, or less than 5. If it is worth more than 5, then it is a better position for white, and black, playing to win, would not take it. If it is worth less than 5, then black will take it, and the result will only be worse for white. Thus, no matter what, if the machine moves to position B, it can expect to end up with a position valued at 5 or less. As it can get 10 by moving to position A, it will never move to B. And it can determine this without ever exploring B2, B3, . . ., B12, or any of their descendants. This powerful idea coupled with other mechanisms enabled the search routines to run hundreds or even thousands of times faster than would have otherwise been possible.

Besides having sophisticated search capability, Samuel's program was the first program that *learned* by itself how to perform a task better. Samuel himself was a mediocre checkers player. But he was a very smart computer scientist. He came up with a method by which the computer could

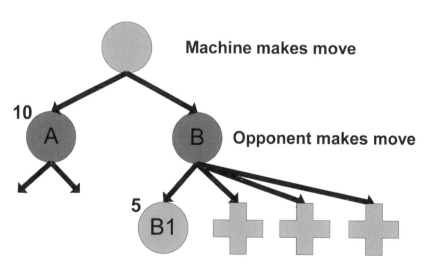

FIGURE 6.4 The alpha-beta search procedure makes move A without examining any of the paths marked +.

gradually improve its play as it played more and more games. Recall that the computer has to evaluate each non-terminal position. One could, for example, count the number of pieces of each type on the board and add them up with appropriate weights. But is a king worth twice as much as a regular piece, or perhaps five times as much? Samuel came up with the following idea: let's learn these weights by seeing which set of weights leads to better play. Thus, the computer would play using one set of weights, and after seeing whether it won or lost the game, it would go and adjust the weights to get a more correct evaluation of the positions it had encountered along the way. If it won, it would aim to increase its valuation for these positions, and if it lost, it would decrease them. Although no single run is reliable in determining the value of a position (a bad position might, by chance, lead to a win), over time the valuations tended to get better. Although the computer started out playing very poor checkers, it ended up playing better than Samuel.

Samuel's program, even today, is a very impressive achievement, since the 701 had 10 kilobytes of main memory and used a magnetic tape (and not a disk) for storage. Thus, it had less memory than one of the musical greeting cards that one can buy at the store for a few dollars.

When it was about to be demonstrated, Thomas J. Watson, Sr., the founder and president of IBM, remarked that the demonstration would raise the price of IBM stock 15 points. It did. Samuel's program and others generated a lot of excitement, and many people were led to believe that computers would soon be better than any human player. Indeed, in 1957, Allen Newell and eventual Nobel-prize winner Herbert Simon predicted that in 10 years, a computer would be world chess champion. Unfortunately, these predictions were premature. Impressive as Samuel's achievement was, it was not a very good checkers player. Although it was able to beat Samuel, most competent checkers players beat it without much strain.

Perhaps an early failure was to be expected in this new science, and people began to write much better programs. This effort was carried over to the more popular game of chess, and a number of individuals around the country began bringing their programs to an annual chess tournament. It was fun to see computers play against each other, but the nagging fact remained: against humans these programs did not offer much competition.

These events led to much thought. What was going on here? The answer seemed to be in the nature of the games of checkers and chess. Researchers realized that the game trees were growing in size at an exponential rate as one looks further ahead in the sequences of possible moves. Computer programs were wasting their time doing a uniform search of every possible move sequence while humans searched only selected paths. Humans had knowledge of which paths were likely to yield interesting results, and they could look much deeper than machines. That is how humans could win.

It seemed obvious that the way to get machines to defeat humans was to design the programs to play more like people: rather than using a lot of computer cycles to explore all these irrelevant paths, the computer should spend more time thinking about which paths to explore. Like people, machines should invest their resources only in selected paths and they should look very far down them. During the 1970s, the annual chess tournament featured many programs that followed this theory: build in a mechanism that simulates a human's ability to search the interesting paths, and create an ability in the machine to see very far into the future moves of the game. It was quite common for program designers to analyze a clever move by their program and brag about the long search that was used to find it. Only a fool who did not understand the modern lessons of game playing would try a uniform search algorithm.

But the next surprise came from a chess program developed at Northwestern University by David Slate, Larry Atkin, and others. They created a uniform search algorithm despite the common wisdom and won the annual tournament. At first, people felt it was just luck, but when the result was repeated a few times, they had to take notice. Why did the uniform search program defy all reason and defeat selected path programs that look much deeper? The answer came from a new rationalization: a program doing uniform search to a fixed depth plays perfectly to that depth. It never makes a mistake. Yet a selective search program does make an occasional mistake within that depth, and when it does the uniform search program grabs the advantage. Usually the advantage is enough to win the game. So uniform search programs dominated the field, and variations on them still are being used.

But the question remained: when would these programs finally become good enough to defeat humans? Although the Simon-Newell prediction asserted 10 years from 1957, the reality was that it took 40 years. A computer first became world champion in 1997, when IBM's Deep Blue defeated Garry Kasparov. In a match that involved six games, Deep Blue won two games, lost one, and tied three. The ultimate goal of a 40-year quest had been achieved. But examine for a moment the computational resources that were brought against the human player. Deep Blue ran on the powerful RS/6000 machine running 32 processors in parallel and also had special-purpose circuitry to generate chess moves. Deep Blue benefited greatly from harnessing Moore's law (see Hill in Chapter 2). This giant machine examined 200 million chess moves per second! But a lot of computer cycles were not the only factor in Deep Blue's victory. The Deep Blue team had spent years building special chess knowledge into the software and hardware of the system, and the system's play had been criticized regularly by chess masters during its development and improved through many redesigns and modifications. Only through this coordinated and long-term effort was the win possible.

The years also proved the importance of the learning techniques developed by Samuel in his checkers program. For example, the world's best backgammon program, one which plays at world-champion level, is a program developed by Gerry Tesauro (also at IBM). The main idea in this program is not search: search does not work well in backgammon, where even a single play of the game involves thousands of different possible successor states. The main idea in this program is a learning algorithm that learns to evaluate the quality of different positions. This program's evaluation was so good that it changed the evaluation of certain positions, and therefore changed the way in which experts play the game!

This story teaches us very much about game playing. But it also teaches us about the nature of computation and the nature of human problem solving. Here are some of the major lessons:

• *Our intuitions and thoughtful insights into a process as complicated as playing one of these board games are very unreliable.* We learn things in information science by writing a program and observing its behavior. We may theorize or estimate or consult our experts at length on some problems, but often we cannot find the answer without doing the experiment. On numerous occasions, we found the experts were wrong and the world of experiment held an amazing lesson for us.

• *The process of decision making in games is vastly more complex than we imagined.* It was a combination of increased computer speed combined with decades of research on search and evaluation methods that eventually made it possible to defeat a great chess champion. It was not clear in the early days how much of either of these—machine speed or quality of search—would be needed, and it is a profound lesson to observe how much of each was required. This provides us with plenty of warning that when we examine other decision processes such as in economic, political, or medical diagnosis situations, we may find similar difficulties.

• *It is not always the case that to achieve human-level performance, a computer should use the same techniques that a human does.* The way a computer does computation is inherently different from the way the brain works, and different approaches might be suitable for these two "computing architectures." However, the performance of Deep Blue also shows that quantity (a large amount of computer cycles) might occasionally lead to quality—a performance that might be at the level of a human, or indeed indistinguishable from that of a human. (In the match between Deep Blue and Kasparov, several of Kasparov's advisors accused IBM of cheating by having human players feeding moves to Deep Blue.) But is this much brute-force computation really necessary in order to play high-quality chess? We have the feeling that there must be a more efficient use of machines that will do the same job. But we have no idea what it is. Perhaps, in order to solve that problem, we need to really understand how intelligence works and how to implement it within a computer.

• *Rather than designing a program in its entirety, it may be better to let the computer learn for itself.* There is a lot of knowledge that people might have based on their experience but do not know how to make explicit. Sometimes there is simply no substitute for hands-on experience, even for a computer.

• *The research in game playing over the years has had ramifications for many other areas of computing.* For example, computer chess research at IBM demonstrated computing technology that has also been used to attack problems related to computations on environmental issues, modeling financial data, the design of automobiles, and the development of innovative drug therapies. Samuel's ideas on how to get programs to improve their performance by learning have provided a basis for tackling applications as diverse as learning to fly a helicopter, learning to search the Web, or learning to plan operations in a large factory.

7

Building Computing Systems of Practical Scale

Computer science values not only fundamental knowledge but also working systems that are widely useful. We deliver the benefits of computer science research through these large-scale, complex computing systems, and their design, development, and deployment constitute a fruitful area of research in itself. In doing so, we often raise new questions about fundamental issues.

Started as an attempt to share scarce computing resources, the Internet has become a ubiquitous global utility service, powering personal and commercial transactions and creating domestic and international policy challenges. Along the way it has provided a testbed for research that ranges from high-speed communication to social interactions to new business models. The remarkable success of the Internet, including its scalability and heterogeneity, results from inspired use of engineering-design principles. Peterson and Clark show how some basic principles of generality, layers of abstraction, codified interfaces, and virtual resources led to a system architecture that has survived many orders of magnitude of growth.

The creators of the Internet did not anticipate—*couldn't* have anticipated—all of its consequences, including the emergence of the World Wide Web as the principal public-access mechanism for the Internet. The World Wide Web emerged through the synergy of universal naming, browsers, widespread convenient Internet access, the Hyper Text Transfer Protocol, a series of markup languages, and the (relative) platform independence of these mechanisms. The Web has presented new opportunities—including support for communication within distributed communities—and it has also led to a number of new problems, not the least of which are security and privacy. Bruckman assesses the emerging use of the Internet as a communication medium that links widely dispersed communities, and she analyzes the factors behind the development of these communities.

Sudan reviews the history of the cryptography and security mechanisms that underlie secure Web protocols and other forms of secure computer communication. Also evident is another example of how new opportunities arise when we find a way to eliminate a significant premise of a technology—in this case, the advance exchange of decryption information, or the codebook. Sudan also shows how the computational paradigm has changed even the basic notion of what constitutes proof in an authentication system.

Software engineering research is concerned with better ways to design, analyze, develop, evaluate, maintain, and evolve the complex systems that deliver the computing services described in Peterson and Clark, Bruckman, and Sudan. Shaw describes how software engineering researchers formulate and evaluate research of this kind and employ a variety of approaches to address the subdiscipline's different types of problems.

THE INTERNET: AN EXPERIMENT THAT ESCAPED
FROM THE LAB

Larry Peterson, Princeton University, and
David Clark, Massachusetts Institute of Technology

The recent explosion of the Internet onto the world's consciousness is one of the most visible successes of the computer science research community. The impact of the Internet in enabling commerce, allowing people to communicate with each other, and connecting us to vast stores of information and entertainment is undeniable. What is surprising to most people who now take the Internet for granted is that the underlying architecture that has allowed the Internet to grow to its current scale was defined over 25 years ago.

This remarkable story began in the late 1970s when a collection of computer science researchers, then numbering less than a hundred, first deployed an experimental packet-switch network on tens of computers connected by 56-kbps links. They built the network with the modest goal of being able to remotely enter jobs on each others' computers, but more importantly, as an experiment to help them better understand the principles of network communication and fault-tolerant communication. Only in their wildest dreams did they imagine that their experiment would enter the mainstream of society, or that over the next 25 years both the bandwidth of its underlying links and the number of users it connects would each grow by six orders of magnitude (to 10-Gbps links and 100 million users, respectively). That a single architecture not only survived this growth, but also in fact enabled it, is a testament to the soundness of its design.

Layering and Abstraction

Several design principles, many of them sharpened by years of experience building early operating systems like Multics, helped shape the Internet architecture.

The most important of these was to employ multiple layers of abstraction (see earlier essays) to manage the complexity of the system. Networks cannot claim to have invented hierarchical abstraction, but they have become the most visible application of layering. At the lowest level, electrical-magnetic signals propagate over some medium, such as a copper wire or an optical fiber. At the next level, bits are encoded onto these signals. Groups of bits are then collected together, so abstractly we can think of machines sending self-contained messages to each other. At the next layer, a sequence of machines forwards these messages along a route from the original source to the ultimate destination. At a still higher layer, the source and destination machines accept and deliver these messages on behalf of application processes that they host. We can think of this layer as providing an abstract channel over which two (or more) processes communicate. Finally, at the highest level, application programs extract meaning from the messages they receive from their peers.

Recognizing that layering is a helpful tool is one thing. Understanding the right layers to define is quite another. Here, the architects of the Internet were guided by another design principle, generalization. One dimension of generalization is to support as many applications as possible, including applications that have not yet been imagined. In terms recognized by all computer scientists, the goal was to build a network that could be programmed for many different purposes. It was not designed to just carry human voice or TV signals, as were other contemporary networks. Instead, one of the main characteristics of the Internet is that through a simple matter of programming, it can support virtually any type of communication service. The other dimension of generality is to accommodate as many underlying communication technologies as possible. This is akin to implementing a universal machine on any number of different computational elements. Looked at another way, the Internet is a purely logical network, implemented primarily in software, and running on top of a wide assortment of physical networks.

Next you need to codify the interfaces to the various layers. Here, early Internet researchers recognized the need to keep the common interfaces minimal, thereby placing the fewest constraints on the future users of the Internet, including both the designers of the underlying technologies upon which it would be built and the programmers that would write the next generation of applications. This allows for autonomy among the entities that connect to the Internet: they can run whatever operating system they want, on whatever hardware they want, as long as they support the agreed upon interface. In this case, the key interface is between code modules running on different machines rather than modules running on the same machine. Such interfaces are commonly called protocols: the set of rules that define what messages can be sent between a pair of machines, and under what circumstances.

In the early days of network design, it was not clear that we could actually write protocol specifications with sufficient clarity and precision that successful communication was practical. In the 1970s it was predicted that the only way to get different computers to communicate with each other was to have a single group of people build the code for all the machines, so that they could take into account all the details that would never be specified properly in practice. Today, the idea that protocols can be well specified is accepted, but a great deal of work went into learning how to do this, including both practical experiments and theoretical work on automatic checking of specifications.

The general idea of abstraction takes many forms in the Internet. In addition to using layering as a technique for managing complexity, a form of abstraction known as hierarchical aggregation is used to manage the Internet's scale. Today, the Internet consists of tens of millions of machines, but these machines cannot possibly all know about each other. How then, can a message be correctly delivered from one machine to another? The answer is that collections of machines are first aggregated according to the physical network segment they are attached to, and then a second time according to the logical segment (autonomous domain) to which they belong. This means that machines are assigned hierarchical addresses, such that finding a path from a source machine to a destination machine reduces to the problem of finding a path to the destination domain, which is then responsible for delivering the data to the right physical segment, and finally to the destination machine. Thus, just as layering involves a high-level protocol hiding the uninteresting details about a low-level protocol, aggregation involves high levels of the addressing and routing hierarchy masking the uninteresting details about lower levels in the hierarchy.

Resource Sharing

Networks are shared systems. Many users send traffic from many applications across the same communication links at the same time. The goal is the efficient exploitation of expensive resources. Long-distance communication links are expensive, and if many people can share them, the cost per user to communicate is greatly reduced.

The telephone system is a shared system, but the sharing occurs at the granularity of a call. When a user attempts to make a call, the network determines if there is capacity available. If so, that capacity is allocated to the caller for as long as the call lasts, which might be minutes or hours. If there is no capacity, the caller is signaled with a busy tone.

Allocating communications capacity for a period of minutes or hours was found to be very inefficient when computer applications communicated. Traffic among computers seems to be very bursty, with short transmissions separated by periods of silence. To carry this traffic efficiently, a much more fine-grained sharing was proposed. The traffic to be sent is broken into small chunks called packets, which contain both data to be sent and delivery information. Packets from many users come together and are transmitted, in turn, across the links in the network from source toward destination.

When the concept of packet was first proposed, there was considerable uncertainty as to whether this degree of multiplexing would work. If traffic from multiple users arrives to be sent at the same instant, a queue of packets must form until all can finally be sent. But if the arrival pattern of packets is unpredictable, is it possible that long, persistent queues will form? Will the resulting system actually be usable? The mathematics of queuing theory were developed to try to understand how such systems might work. Queuing theory, of course, is not restricted to network design. It applies to checkout lines in stores, hospital emergency rooms, and any other situation where arrival patterns and service times are predictable only in a statistical sense. But network design has motivated a great deal of research that has taught us much about statistical properties of shared systems. We now know the conditions to build systems like this with predictable stability, reasonable traffic loads, and support for a wide range of applications. The concept of the packet has turned out to be a very robust one that has passed the test of time.

More recently, as the Internet has grown larger, and the number of interacting traffic flows has grown, a new set of observations have emerged. The Internet seems to display traffic patterns that are self-similar, which means that the patterns of bursts that we see in the aggregated traffic have the same appearance when viewed at different time scales. This hints that the mathematics of chaos theory may be the tool of choice to increase our understanding of how these large, shared systems work.

Devising techniques to share resources is a recurring problem in computer science. In the era of expensive processors, time-sharing systems were developed to share them. Cheaper processors brought the personal computer, which attempts to side-step some of the harder sharing problems by giving each user his own machine. But sharing is a fundamental aspect of networking, because sharing and communication among people and the computers that serve them is a fundamental objective. So mastery of the models, tools, and methods to think about sharing is a fundamental objective of computer science.

Concluding Remarks

The Internet is arguably the largest man-made information system ever deployed, as measured by the number of users and the amount of data sent over it, as well as in terms of the heterogeneity it accommodates, the number of state transitions that are possible, and the number of autonomous domains it permits. What's more, it is only going to grow in size and coverage as sensors, embedded devices, and consumer electronic equipment become connected. Although there have certainly been stresses on the architecture, in every case so far the keepers of the Internet have been able to change the implementation while leaving the architecture and interfaces virtually unchanged. This is a testament to the soundness of the architecture, which at its core defines a "universal network machine."

By locking down the right interfaces, but leaving the rest of the requirements underspecified, the Internet has evolved in ways never imagined. Certainly this is reflected in the set of applications that run on the Internet, ranging from video conferencing to e-commerce, but it is also now the case that the Internet has grown to be so complicated that the computer scientists that created it can no longer fully explain or predict its behavior. In effect, the Internet has become like a natural organism that can only be understood through experimentation, and even though it is a deterministic system, researchers are forced to create models of its behavior, just as scientists model the physical world. In the end, the Internet must be viewed as an information phenomenon: one that is capable of supporting an ever-changing set of applications, and whose behavior can be understood only through the use of increasingly sophisticated measurement tools and predictive models.

MANY-TO-MANY COMMUNICATION: A NEW MEDIUM

Amy Bruckman, Georgia Institute of Technology

In the early 1990s, computer-mediated communication (CMC) exploded in popularity, moving from a tool used by small groups of engineers and scientists to a mass phenomenon affecting nearly every aspect of life in industrialized nations. Even in the developing world, CMC has begun to play a significant role. Yet we are just at the beginning, not the end, of the transformations catalyzed by this technology. We can draw an analogy to an earlier era of intense social change launched by new technology: the introduction of the car. In the early days of the internal combustion engine, cars were called "horseless carriages": we understood the new technology in terms of an old, familiar one. At that stage, we could not begin to imagine the ways that cars would transform the United States and the world, both for good and for ill. The Internet is in its "horseless carriage" stage. At this pivotal moment, we have a unique opportunity to shape the technology's evolution, and the inevitable changes to society that will accompany it.

The key feature of this technology is its support for many-to-many communications. This paper will analyze the significance of many-to-many communications in key relevant application areas.

With many-to-many communications, individuals are becoming creators of content, not merely recipients. For example, we are no longer restricted to reading journalistic interpretations of current events, but can now also share our own views with friends and family. Opportunities for discourse on issues of import are at the foundation of a democratic society. We are experiencing a renaissance in public debate of serious matters by citizens.

Many-to-many communications are changing the nature of medicine. The new medical consumer arrives at the doctor's office better informed. The Pew Center for Internet Life reports that "fifty-two million American adults, or 55% of those with Internet access, have used the Web to get health or medical information," and of those, "70% said the Web information influenced their decision about how to treat an illness or condition" (Fox and Rainie, 2000). Patients can talk online with others with similar ailments, exchanging not just useful medical information but also emotional support. This emotional support is particularly valuable to caregivers of patients with serious illnesses, a group whose needs are often neglected.

Many-to-many communications are having a growing impact on business practices. In the field of retailing, consumers can now easily share product recommendations, giving developers of quality products a competitive advantage. Competitive price information is available with unprecedented ease of access. The free many-to-many flow of information moves us closer to the ideal of an efficient market.

New kinds of commerce are emerging. We are no longer bound to have all purchases of second-hand goods go through middlemen like consignment shops, but can sell items directly to others. For example, in areas like antiques, collectibles, and used consumer electronics, for the first time in history a fair and efficient market has emerged. Items that would otherwise have been discarded can now find their way to just the person who needs them, leading to a less wasteful society.

The remainder of this paper discusses three application areas where the impact of Internet technology merits special attention: the expansion of scientific knowledge, entertainment, and education.

Accelerating the Expansion of Knowledge

The Internet's most obvious capability is to distribute information. The World Wide Web was invented by Tim Berners-Lee and colleagues at CERN in order to accelerate scientific progress: researchers can exchange ideas must faster than was formerly possible. This has had particular impact in the developing world. Researchers in developing nations who could never afford subscriptions to research journals now have growing access to current scientific information and indirect participation in the international community of scientists.

Sociologists of science like Bruno Latour teach us that truth is socially constructed. This is true of the most basic "hard" scientific facts. A new idea begins attributed to a specific person: "Einstein says that $E = MC^2$." As it becomes more accepted, the attribution is dropped to a footnote: "$E = MC^2$ (Einstein 1905)." Finally, the attribution is deemed entirely unnecessary, and one can simply say "$E = MC^2$"—it has become an accepted scientific fact (Latour et al., 1986). The process of one researcher's claim rising to the level of fact is fundamentally social. Initially, people are unsure—was the scientist's work sound? Do others support this finding? As such questions are asked and answered, some claims are rejected and others become widely accepted. Truth emerges not from the work of one scientist, but from the community. It is not instantly revealed, but begins as tentative and solidifies over time. The Internet gets the most attention for its ability to support the exchange of factual information in the simple sense, as if it is merely a giant database that is unusually up to date. However, it is important to understand Latour's subtler vision of how new knowledge is constructed, and the way that the Internet is uniquely well suited to accelerating that social process.

As we move forward, we need to find ways to enhance the ability of network technology to facilitate the free exchange of scientific ideas. Academic researchers in most fields are still rewarded for presenting ideas in peer-reviewed journal articles that may take years to appear in print. They are often reluctant to share ideas before they appear in officially credited form. Corporate researchers may be reluctant to share findings at all. Yet the entire endeavor of research can be enhanced through more immediate sharing of ideas via the Internet. The challenge, then, is to find ways to give individuals credit for ideas shared rapidly online, while at the same time maintaining the quality control of peer review. The field of online community research focuses on these issues, especially, what motivates individuals to contribute and how quality of discourse can be maintained (Preece, 2000). The design of our next-generation communication systems will help to accelerate the pace of discovery in all fields.

Online Entertainment

As we have seen, we can view the Internet as facilitating the exchange of scientific information; however, it is more far-reaching to see it as supporting the growth of a community of scientists (and information as a key product of that community). This fundamental insight applies not just to science, but to most domains. For example, the entertainment industry is no longer simply delivering content, but is using computer networks to bring groups of individuals together. New Internet-based forms of entertainment fall into a variety of genres, including bulletin-board systems (BBSs), chat, and games.

Internet-based communication provides opportunities for new kinds of socializing. In chat rooms and on BBSs, people gather together to discuss hobbies and to meet others. People with an unusual hobby find they are no longer alone but can meet like-minded others from around the world. Some of this social activity bridges into face-to-face activity. Hobbyists from geographically diverse areas may meet face to face at annual conventions and then maintain those ties online. In other cases, the social activity is local in nature. Computer-mediated communication is used to schedule face-to-face meetings and to continue discussion between such meetings. Sociologist Robert Putnam has documented a decrease in Americans' participation in civic groups over the last half-century (Putnam, 1995). The ease of coordinating social and civic groups with the aid of new communications technologies has the potential to help begin to reverse this trend.

Popular types of Internet-based games include traditional games (like bridge and chess), fantasy sports, action games, and massively multi-player games (MMPs). The most important characteristic these games share is that they are social: people play with relatives, old friends, and new friends met online. For example, the author plays bridge online with her mother (who lives hundreds of miles away) and action games with friends from high school and graduate school living all around the country. Getting together to play online gives us occasions to keep in touch. This new entertainment form can help to maintain what sociologists call "strong ties" over distance and also create new "weak ties" (Wellman and Gulia, 1999). While one might be inclined to dismiss friendships made online as trivial, they are often quite meaningful to participants and sometimes have practical value as well. Howard Rheingold recounts how people who know one another from a California BBS called The WELL sent hundreds of books to a book-loving group member who lost all his possessions in a fire. WELL members also collaborated to arrange for the medical evacuation of a group member who became ill while in the Himalayas (Rheingold, 1993). These kinds of stories are not unusual. Every year, students in the "Design of Online Communities" graduate class at Georgia Tech are asked to write a short essay on their best and worst experiences involving Internet-based communications, and similar stories emerge each time.

It's important to note that a number of aspects of online entertainment are discouraging. In particular, some online games are so compelling for many players that they may devote extremely large amounts of time to playing them. For example, as of fall 2001, the most popular MMP— Everquest, by Verant Interactive—had 400,000 registered members (Verant, 2001) who spent on average 22.5 hours per week playing (Yee, 2001). That mean figure includes a significant number who hardly participate at all, so the median is likely substantially higher. In other words, there are tens and possibly hundreds of thousands of people who devote all their non-work time to participation in the game. While we must be careful about passing judgement on how others spend their free time, the players themselves often find this problematic—so much so that the game is often referred to by the nickname "EverCrack." Other games in this new genre have similar holding power.

MMPs are fun for players and profitable for game companies. In addition to charging people to buy the game initially, companies also charge a monthly fee. This lets companies make more money from a single development effort and gives them a more even revenue stream, making them less dependent on unpredictable seasonal sales and new releases. As a result, many companies are developing new MMP titles. While traditional multiplayer games allow a handful of people to interact in the same game space, MMPs support thousands. It's likely we are just at the beginning of their growth in popularity. While they provide an entertainment offering that is both social and active, they also tend to lead to overinvolvement by some players. This is a key moment to ask: How can we shape this trend? How should we?

One constructive course of action is to create game-like environments that have educational content. For example, "AquaMOOSE 3D" is a three-dimensional virtual world designed to help high-school students learn mathematics (Edwards et al., 2001). See Figure 7.1. You are a fish, and you specify your motion in the graphical world mathematically. For example, swim in a sine in x and a cosine in y, and you move in a spiral and leave a spiral trail behind you. You can also create sets of rings in the water and challenge others to guess the equation that goes through them. Students create these mathematical puzzles to challenge their friends. AquaMOOSE looks much like the purely entertainment environments many students find so compelling, but time spent there is educationally valuable. We need to develop more such environments to encourage students to choose to spend their free time wisely.

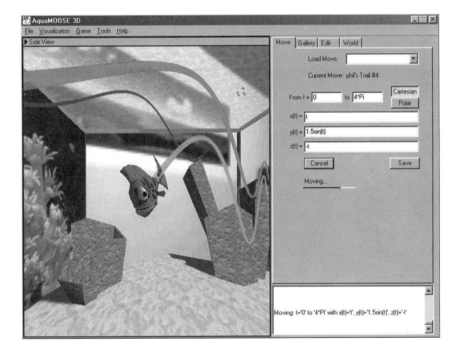

FIGURE 7.1 "AquaMOOSE 3D": An Internet-based math-learning environment.

The Learning Potential of Internet Technology

Education is a key area where many-to-many communications have begun to have a strong positive impact. Many educational applications of Internet technology focus on information: in distance education information is delivered to the student. In online research projects, information is retrieved. In more innovative work, information is gathered by students and shared. While information-oriented applications of Internet technology are useful, the more exciting potential of this new learning medium is not about information but about community and collaboration. Online, groups of learners can motivate and support one another's learning experiences.

Learning from Peers

Learning is fundamentally a social process, and the Internet has a unique potential to facilitate new kinds of learning relationships. For example, in the "One Sky, Many Voices" project by Nancy Songer at the University of Michigan (http://www.onesky.umich.edu/), kids can learn about atmospheric phenomena from scientists working in the field (Songer, 1996). More importantly, the students also learn from one another: kids in Montana studying hurricanes can talk online with Florida students in the midst of one. Learning from peers can be a compelling experience and is a scalable educational solution. If enough educational programs try to leverage the skills of adult experts, experts will ultimately spend all their time in public service. While the supply of experts is limited, the supply of peers is not.

Peers can be a powerful resource for children's learning, if activities are structured to promote productive interactions. MOOSE Crossing is a text-based virtual world (or "MUD") in which kids 8 to 13 years old learn creative writing and object-oriented programming from one another (http://www.cc.gatech.edu/elc/moose-crossing/). See Figure 7.2. The specially designed programming language (MOOSE) and environment (MacMOOSE and WinMOOSE) make it easy for young kids to learn to program. Members don't just experience the virtual world—they construct it collaboratively. For example, Carrot[1] (girl, age 9) created a swimming pool complex. Using lists stored on properties of the pool object, she keeps track of who is in the pool, sauna, or Jacuzzi, and who has changed into a bathing suit. You obviously can't jump into the pool if you're

---

[1]All real names and online pseudonyms of participants have been changed to protect their confidentiality.

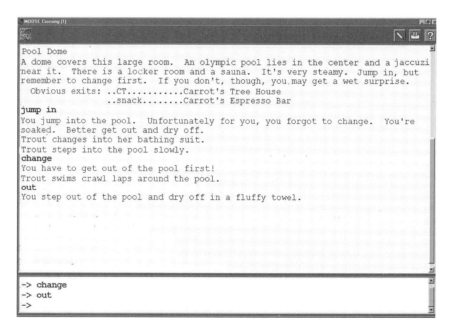

```
MOOSE Crossing [1]

Pool Dome
A dome covers this large room.  An olympic pool lies in the center and a jaccuzi
near it.  There is a locker room and a sauna.  It's very steamy.  Jump in, but
remember to change first.  If you don't, though, you.may get a wet surprise.
  Obvious exits: ..CT..........Carrot's Tree House
                 ..snack........Carrot's Espresso Bar
jump in
You jump into the pool.  Unfortunately for you, you forgot to change.  You're
soaked.  Better get out and dry off.
Trout changes into her bathing suit.
Trout steps into the pool slowly.
change
You have to get out of the pool first!
Trout swims crawl laps around the pool.
out
You step out of the pool and dry off in a fluffy towel.




-> change
-> out
->
```

FIGURE 7.2 A text-based virtual world where kids practice creative writing and learn object-oriented programming.

already in the water . . . you need to get out first! This gives Carrot opportunities for comic writing as well as programming. The text-based nature of the environment is not a technical limitation, but rather a deliberate design choice: it gives kids a context for using language playfully and imaginatively. Carrot enjoys inviting other kids over to the pool. They in turn learn about programming and writing using her work as a model (Bruckman, 1998, 2000).

The online community provides a ready source of peer support for learning. Kids learn from one another, and from one another's projects. That support is not just technical, but also emotional. In answering a question, one child may tell another, "I got confused by that too at first." The online community provides a ready source of role models. If, for example, girls are inclined to worry that programming might not be a cool thing for a girl to do, they are surrounded by girls and women engaging in this activity successfully and enjoying it. Finally, the online community provides an appreciative audience for completed work. Kids get excited about being creative in order to share their work with their peers.

Elders as Mentors

Social support for learning online can come not just from peers, teachers, and experts, but also from ordinary members of the general population, who form a vast potential resource for our children's education. Retired people in particular have a great deal they can teach kids and free time to contribute, but they need an easy and well-structured way to do so. In the Palaver Tree Online project (http://www.cc.gatech.edu/elc/palaver/, the dissertation research of Georgia Tech PhD student Jason Ellis), middle-school students learn about history from elders who lived through it. Teachers begin with literature that is part of their normal curriculum. Kids brainstorm historical questions based on what they've learned, interview elder mentors about their personal experiences with that time, and then write research reports about what they've learned. See Figures 7.3 and 7.4. In our studies to date, kids learning about World War II interviewed veterans, and kids learning about the civil rights years interviewed older African Americans. History learned from real people becomes more meaningful and relevant (Ellis and Bruckman, 2001).

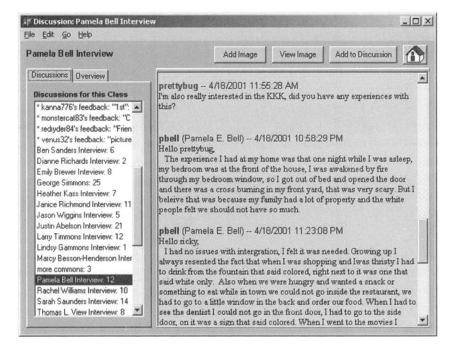

FIGURE 7.3 Eighth-grade students interviewing an elder mentor about her experiences growing up during the civil rights years. (All names have been changed.)

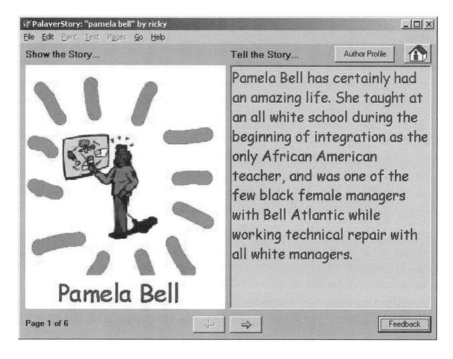

FIGURE 7.4 The project students created based on their interview.

Of course it would be better for kids to meet with elders face to face, but in practice this rarely if ever happens. In interviews with teachers who have tried such projects, we found that the logistics are too difficult to arrange for all involved. Elder volunteers, when asked if they will drive to an unfamiliar place and commit to multiple visits, often hesitate. However, when asked, "Would you be willing to log on for half an hour a day for a few weeks?," they are enthusiastic. The Palaver Tree Online community makes this not only possible but also relatively easy for the elders, students, and teachers. Teachers are already overwhelmed with work, and any successful school-based learning technology needs to make their lives easier, not harder.

New Social and Technical Possibilities

Culture and technology co-evolve. The challenge as we move forward is to develop a vision of what is possible—to understand the more and less desirable outcomes, and try to steer in the right direction. Hardware and software infrastructure developed over the last 40 years are just now becoming widely available and are finding a wide variety of new applications. The wide availability of Internet access has made many-to-many communications possible, and this capability has a profound impact on how we conduct business, manage our health, share knowledge, entertain ourselves and one another, and learn.

References

Bruckman, A., 1998, "Community Support for Constructionist Learning," *Computer Supported Cooperative Work* 7:47-86.

Bruckman, A., 2000, "Situated Support for Learning: Storm's Weekend with Rachael," *Journal of the Learning Sciences* 9(3):329-372.

Edwards, E., J. Elliott, and A. Bruckman, 2001, "AquaMOOSE 3D: Math Learning in a 3D Multi-user Virtual World," paper presented at the CHI 2001 Conference on Human Factors in Computing Systems, Seattle, Wash.

Ellis, J., and A. Bruckman, 2001, "Palaver Tree Online: Supporting Social Roles in a Community of Oral History," paper presented at the CHI 2001 Conference on Human Factors in Computing Systems, Seattle, Wash.

Fox, S., and L. Rainie, 2000, *The Online Health Care Revolution: How the Web Helps Americans Take Better Care of Themselves,* Pew Internet and American Life Project, Washington, D.C.

Latour, B., S. Woolgar, and J. Salk, 1986, *Laboratory Life,* Princeton University Press, Princeton, N.J.

Preece, J., 2000, *Online Communities: Designing Usability, Supporting Sociability,* John Wiley & Sons, New York.

Putnam, R., 1995, "Bowling Alone: America's Declining Social Capital," *Journal of Democracy* 6(1).

Rheingold, H., 1993, *The Virtual Community: Homesteading on the Electronic Frontier,* Addison-Wesley, Reading, Mass.

Songer, N., 1996, "Exploring Learning Opportunities in Coordinated Network-Enhanced Classrooms: A Case of Kids as Global Scientists," *The Journal of the Learning Sciences* 5(4):297-327.

Verant, 2001, "Sony Online Entertainment to Introduce New EverQuest Servers in European Markets: Verant Interactive."

Wellman, B., and M. Gulia, 1999, "Virtual Communities Are Communities: Net Surfers Don't Ride Alone," in M.A. Smith and P. Kollock (eds.), *Communities in Cyberspace,* Routledge, New York.

Yee, N., 2001, "The Norrathian Scrolls: A Study of Everquest (2.5)," available at http://www.nickyee.com/eqt/report.html.

CRYPTOGRAPHY

Madhu Sudan, Massachusetts Institute of Technology

Consider the following prototypical scenario in the Internet era: Alice wishes to access her bank account with the Bank of Billionaires (Bob) through the Internet. She wishes to transmit to Bob her account number and password and yet does not want her Internet service provider to know her account number and password. The potential for commerce over the Internet relies critically on the ability to implement this simple scenario. Yet when one gets down to formalizing the goals of this scenario mathematically, one realizes this goal is almost impossible. After all the Internet service provider has access to every bit of information that enters or leaves Alice's computer, and Bob has only a subset! Fortunately, there is a tiny crack in any such "proof" of impossibility (read "Computational Foundations of Cryptography" below for details)—a crack visible only when inspected with a computational lens—and from this crack emerges *cryptography*, the science of encrypting and decrypting messages.

Cryptography has been practiced for centuries now. Its need becomes evident in any situation involving long-distance communication where secrecy and (mis)trust are governing factors. Yet, till the advent of the 20th century much of cryptography has been misunderstood and practiced as "black magic" rather than as a science. The advent of computers, and the development of the computational perspective, has changed all this. Today, one can deal with the subject with all the rigor and precision associated with all other mathematical subjects. Achieving this progress has required the formalization of some notions—such as randomness, knowledge, and proof—that we rely on commonly in our lives but whose mathematical formalization seems very elusive. It turns out that all these notions are essentially computational, as is cryptography. Furthermore cryptography is feasible only if some very fundamental computational hypotheses (such as NP P; see Kleinberg and Papadimitriou in Chapter 2) hold out. This essay describes some of the salient events in the history of cryptography.

Cryptography in the Medieval Era

Traditionally, messages were encrypted with codebooks. Roughly, in this setup Alice and Bob initially share some secret information, called the codebook. This codebook might be something as simple as a letter-to-letter substitution rule, or something more complex—such as a word-to-word substitution rule, and so on. When Alice obtains some new information to be transmitted secretly to Bob, she uses the codebook to translate the message and send it (through untrusted couriers) to the receiver. Now, assuming that the courier does deliver the encrypted message, the receiver uses his copy of the codebook to translate the messages back. The courier or any other eavesdropper, however, cannot in theory decipher the message, since he does not possess the codebook.

To compare the above system with some of the more recent themes in cryptography, let us compare some of the basic elements of the model and the associated assumptions. One of the primary features of the model above is the role of the codebook. It is what distinguishes the receiver from the eavesdropper (based on information the receiver possesses), and the initial cryptography protocols assumed (mistakenly, as it turned out) that the codebook was a necessary component for secret communication. Over time, the belief took on quantitative dimensions—the larger the size of the codebook, the more secure the encryption. For example, a letter-to-letter substitution rule applied to the English alphabet requires the testing of 26! possibilities. But most can be ruled out easily based on frequency analysis of English text. So letter-to-letter substitution rules, involving small codebooks, can be broken easily. Word-to-word substitution rules are harder to break, but it is still feasible to do so with decent computers.

The last of these observations, that better computers might lead to loss of secrecy, was worrisome. Maybe the advent of computers would lead to the ultimate demise of cryptography! In the face of such popular beliefs, it came as a startling surprise that cryptography could potentially thrive with advances in computing.

Computational Foundations of Cryptography

The foundations of cryptography were laid gradually. First came information-theoretic foundations, starting with Shannon in the 1950s, and a little later, in the 1970s, came the computational notions of Merkle (1978), Diffie and Hellman (1976), and Rivest, Shamir, and Adleman (1978).

Shannon's theory (Shannon, 1949) formally asserted that secret communication is possible whenever the communicating parties, Alice and Bob, share some secret information. Furthermore, this secret information had to have some randomness associated with it, in order to prove the security of the transmission. Quantifying this notion (how random is the shared secret?) led to a quantification of how much information could be exchanged secretly. In particular, if Alice and Bob got together and picked a k-bit random string as the secret to share (where every bit is chosen uniformly and independent of other bits), then Alice could encrypt any k-bit message and send the encrypted message to Bob in the clear, such that the eavesdropper could get no information about the message while

Bob, with knowledge of the shared secret, could decrypt the message from the encrypted form. (For example, if the shared secret s is interpreted as a k-bit integer and the message m to be exchanged is also a k-bit integer, then the encrypted text can simply be $e = (m + s) \bmod 2^k$. Bob, on receiving e, can recover m by computing $e - s \bmod 2^k$).

The importance of this result is not so much in the protocol derived as in the notions defined. How do we determine secrecy? Why is the message m being kept secret in the above exchange? How do we prove it? The answers all turn out to be quite simple. Message m is secret because its encryption (which is a random variable dependent on the secret s) is distributed statistically identically to the encryption of some other message m'. Thus indistinguishability is the basis for secrecy.

What happens when Alice tries to transmit a message of more than k-bits to Bob (while they only share a k-bit secret)? Shannon's theory explained that in this case the eavesdropper can get some information about the message m from the transmission (no matter what protocol Alice and Bob adopt). Shannon realized that this information may not provide any "usable" information about the message itself, but he was unable to exploit this lack of "usability" any further.

How is it possible that one has information about some string m, but is not able to use it? How does one determine "usability" so as to have a meaningful sense of this possibility? It turns out that these questions are essentially computational, and it took the seminal work of Diffie and Hellman (1976) to realize the computational underpinnings and to exploit them.

Diffie and Hellman noticed that several forms of computation transform meaningful information into incomprehensible forms. (As a side remark they note that small programs written in a high-level language immediately reveal their purpose, whereas once they are compiled into a low-level language it is hard to figure out what the program is doing!) They pointed out a specific algebraic computation that seems to have this very useful "information-hiding" feature. They noticed it is very easy to compute modular exponentiation. In particular, given an n-bit prime number p, an integer g between 2 and $p - 1$, and exponent x between 1 and $p - 1$, it is possible to compute $y = g^x \pmod p$ in approximately n^2 steps of computation. Furthermore if g is chosen somewhat carefully, then this mapping from x to $g^x \pmod p$ is one to one and thus invertible. However, no computationally efficient procedure was known (then or now) to compute, given g, p, and y, an integer x such that $y = g^x$. This task of inverting modular exponentiation is referred to as the Discrete Logarithm Problem.

Relying in part on the seeming hardness of the Discrete Log Problem, Diffie and Hellman suggested the following possibility for Alice and Bob to exchange secrets: to exchange an n-bit secret Alice picks a prime p and an integer g as above and sends g and p (in the clear!) to Bob. She then picks a random integer x_1 between 1 and $p - 1$, computes $g^{x_1} \bmod p$, and sends this string to Bob. Bob responds by picking another random string x_2 and sending to Alice the string $g^{x_2} \bmod p$. At this point, Alice and Bob can both compute $g^{x_1 x_2} \bmod p$. (Alice computes this as $(g^{x_2})^{x_1}$, while Bob computes this as $(g^{x_1})^{x_2}$).

What about the eavesdropper? Surprisingly, though all this conversation was totally in the clear, the eavesdropper seems to have no efficient way to compute $g^{x_1 x_2}$. She knows g^{x_1} and g^{x_2} but these do not suffice to give an efficient way to compute $g^{x_1 x_2}$. (In all cases we don't know that there is no efficient way to compute one of the unobvious cases—it is just that we don't know of any efficient way to compute them and thus conjecture that these computations are hard.) Thus Alice and Bob have managed to share a "random secret" by communication in the clear that Alice can now use to send the real message m to Bob.

The protocol above provides a simple example of the distinction between information and its usability. Together, g^{x_1} and g^{x_2} specify $g^{x_1 x_2}$ but not in any usable way, it seems. The essence of this distinction is a computational one. And it leads to a very computational framework for cryptography. The protocol can be used to exchange information secretly, where secrecy is now determined using a computational notion of indistinguishability, where computational indistinguishability suggests that no *efficient* algorithm can distinguish between a transcript of a conversation that exchanges a secret m and one that exchanges a secret m'. (Giving a precise formulation is slightly out of scope.)

And what does one gain from this computational insight? For the first time, we have a protocol for exchanging secrets without any prior sharing of secret information (under some computational hardness assumptions).

Lessons Learned from Cryptography

The seminal work of Diffie and Hellman altered fundamental beliefs about secrecy. The natural guess is that any information that Bob may possess unknown to Alice would be useless in preserving the secrecy of a communication from Alice to Bob. A continuation of this line of reasoning leads to the belief that Alice can't send secret information to Bob unless they shared some secrets initially. Yet the above protocol altered this belief totally. The intractability of reversing some forms of computations can lead to secret communication. Such intractability itself relies on some other fundamental questions about computation (and in particular implies P NP). In fact, it was the emerging belief in the conjecture "P NP" that led Diffie and Hellman to propose the possibility of such public-key exchange protocols and posit the possibility of other public-key encryption systems.

In the numerous years since, cryptography has led to numerous computational realizations of conventional wisdom (and "computational" refutations of mathematical truths!). Numerous notions underlying day-to-day phenomena, for which formalization had earlier proved elusive, have now been formalized. Two striking examples of such notions are those of "pseudo-randomness" and "proofs." We discuss these below.

Shannon's theory had asserted that sharing a secret "random" string was necessary for a message to be secure. The Diffie-Hellman protocol managed to evade this requirement by showing how Alice and Bob could create a secret that they shared using public conversations only. This secret was the string $g^{x_1 x_2}$. How random is this secret? The answer depends on your foundations. Information theory would declare this string to be totally "non-random" (or deterministic) given g^{x_1} and g^{x_2}. Computational theory, however, seems to suggest there is some element of randomness to this string. In particular, the triples (g^{x_1}; g^{x_2}; g^{x_3}) and (g^{x_1}; g^{x_2}; $g^{x_1 x_2}$) seem to contain the same amount of randomness, to any computationally bounded program that examines these triples, when x_1; x_2; x_3 are chosen at random independent of each other. So the computational theory allows certain (distribution on) strings to look more random than they are. Such a phenomenon is referred to as pseudo-randomness and was first formalized by Blum and Micali (1984). Pseudo-randomness provides a formal basis for a common (and even widely exploited) belief that simple computational steps can produce a long sequence of "seemingly" uncorrelated or random data. It also provided a fundamental building block that has since been shown to be the crux of much of cryptography.

A second example of a computational phenomenon is the age-old notion of a proof. What is a proof? Turn-of-the-20th-century logicians had grappled with this question successfully and emerged with a clean explanation. A proof is a sequence of simple assertions that concludes with the theorem by which each assertion can be easily verified. The term "easily" here requires a computational formalism, and in fact, this led to the definition of a Turing machine in the 1940s (see Kleinberg and Papadimitriou in Chapter 2). The advent of cryptography leads us back to the notion of a proof and some seemingly impossible tasks. To see the need for this notion, let us revisit the scenario introduced in the opening paragraph. The goal of the scenario can be reinterpreted as follows: Bob knows that Alice is the (only) person who knows a secret password m. So when some user comes along claiming to be Alice, Bob asks for her password, in effect saying *"Prove you are Alice!"* or equivalently *"Prove you know m."* In traditional scenarios Alice would have simply typed out her password m

on her keyboard and sent it over the Internet. This would have corresponded to our standard intuition of a "proof." Unfortunately this standard notion is a replayable one—any eavesdropper could listen in to the conversation and then also prove that he/she is Alice (or knows m). But the interaction above allows Alice to prove to Bob that she knows m (indeed she essentially sends it to him), without revealing m to the eavesdropper. So it seems Alice was able to prove her identity without revealing so much information that others can later prove they are Alice! How did we manage this? The most significant step here is that we changed our notion of a proof. Conventional proofs are passive written texts. The new notion is an "interactive randomized conversation." The new notion, proposed by Goldwasser, Micali, and Rackoff (1989), retains the power of conviction that conventional proofs carry, but it allows for a greater level of secrecy. Proofs can no longer be replayed. As subsequent developments revealed, these proofs also tend to be much shorter and can be verified much more efficiently. So once again computational perspectives significantly altered conventional beliefs.

The Future of Cryptography

Cryptography offers a wonderful example of a phenomenon quite commonplace in the science of computing. The advent of the computer raises a new challenge. And the science rises to meet the new challenge by creating a rich mathematical structure to study, analyze, and solve the new problems. The solutions achieved (and their deployment in almost every existing Web browser!) as well as the scientific knowledge gained ("proofs," "pseudo-randomness," "knowledge") testify to the success of cryptography so far. Going into the future one expects many further challenges as the scope of cryptography broadens and our desire to "go online" increases. One of the biggest challenges thus far has been in creating large, possibly distributed, systems that address the security of their contents. Cryptography may be likened to the task of designing secure locks and keys. No matter how inventive and successful one is with this aspect, it does not automatically lead to secure houses. Similarly, building secure computer systems involves many more challenges in terms of defining goals, making sure they are feasible, and then attaining them efficiently. Research in this direction is expected to be highly active.

To conclude on a somewhat cautious note: Cryptography, like many other scientific developments, faces the problem of being a double-edged sword. Just as it can be used to preserve the privacy of honest individuals, so can it equally well preserve the privacy of the communications of "bad guys." Indeed, fear of this phenomenon has led to government oversight on the use and spread of cryptography and has raised a controversial question: Is the negative impact sufficient to start imposing curbs on cryptographic research? Hopefully, the description above is convincing with respect to two aspects: cryptographic research is essentially just discovering a natural, though surprising, computational phenomenon. Curbing cryptographic research will only create a blind spot in our understanding of this remarkable phenomenon. And while the tools that the research invents end up being powerful with some potential for misuse, knowing the exact potential and limits of these tools is perhaps the best way to curb their misuse. Keeping this in mind, one hopes that cryptographic research can continue to thrive in the future uninhibited by external pressures.

REFERENCES

Blum, Manuel, and Silvio Micali, 1984, "How to Generate Cryptographically Strong Sequences of Pseudorandom Bits," *SIAM Journal on Computing* 13:850-864.

Diffie, Whitfield, and Martin E. Hellman, 1976, "New Directions in Cryptography," *IEEE Transactions on Information Theory* 22(6):644-654.

Goldwasser, Shafi, Silvio Micali, and Charles Rackoff, 1989, "The Knowledge Complexity of Interactive Proof Systems," *SIAM Journal on Computing* 18(1):186-208.

Merkle, Ralph, 1978, "Secure Communications over Insecure Channels," *Communications of the ACM* (April):294-299.

Rivest, Ronald L., Adi Shamir, and Leonard Adleman, 1978, "A Method for Obtaining Digital Signatures and Public-key Cryptosystems," *Communications of the ACM* 21(2):120-126.

Shannon, Claude E., 1949, "Communication Theory of Secrecy Systems," *Bell Systems Technical Journal* 28(6):656-715.

STRATEGIES FOR SOFTWARE ENGINEERING RESEARCH

Mary Shaw, Carnegie Mellon University

Software engineering is the branch of computer science that creates practical, cost-effective solutions to computation and information processing problems, preferentially applying scientific knowledge, developing[2] software systems in the service of mankind. Like all engineering, software engineering entails making decisions under constraints of limited time, knowledge, and resources. The distinctive character of software—the form of the engineered artifact is intangible and discrete—raises special issues of the following kind about its engineering:

• Software is design-intensive; manufacturing costs are a very small component of product costs.

• Software is symbolic, abstract, and more constrained by intellectual complexity than by fundamental physical laws.

• Software engineering is particularly concerned with software that evolves over a long useful lifetime, that serves critical functions, that is embedded in complex software-intensive systems, or that is otherwise used by people whose attention lies appropriately with the application rather than the software itself. These problems are often incompletely defined, lack clear criteria for success, and interact with other difficult problems—the sorts of problems that Rittel and Webber dubbed "wicked problems."[3]

Software engineering rests on three principal intellectual foundations. The principal foundation is a body of *core computer science concepts* relating to data structures, algorithms, programming languages and their semantics, analysis, computability, computational models, and so on; this is the core content of the discipline. The second is a body of *engineering knowledge* related to architecture, the process of engineering, tradeoffs and costs, conventionalization and standards, quality and assurance, and others; this provides the approach to design and problem solving that

---

[2]"Develop"—Software engineering lacks a verb that covers all the activities associated with a software product, from conception through client negotiation, design, implementation, validation, operation, evolution, and other maintenance. Here, "develop" refers inclusively to all those activities. This is less than wholly satisfactory, but it isn't as bad as listing several verbs at every occurrence.

[3]Horst Rittel and Melvin Webber, 1973, "Dilemmas in a General Theory of Planning," *Policy Sciences* 4:155-169, Elsevier Scientific Publishing, Amsterdam.

respects the pragmatic issues of the applications. The third is the *human and social context* of the engineering effort, which includes the process of creating and evolving artifacts, as well as issues related to policy, markets, usability, and socio-economic impacts; this context provides a basis for shaping the engineered artifacts to be fit for their intended use.

Software engineering is often—inappropriately—confused with mere programming or with software management. Both associations are inappropriate, as the responsibilities of an engineer are aimed at the purposeful creation and evolution of software that satisfies a wide range of technical, business, and regulatory requirements—not simply the ability to create code that satisfies these criteria or to manage a project in an orderly, predictable fashion.

Software Engineering

A physicist approaches problems (not just physical problems) by trying to identify masses and forces. A mathematician approaches problems (even the same problems) by trying to identify functional elements and relations. An electrical engineer approaches problems by trying to identify the linearly independent underlying components that can be composed to solve the problem. A programmer views problems operationally, looking for state, sequence, and processes. Here we try to capture the characteristic mind-set of a software engineer.

Computer Science Fundamentals

The core body of systematic knowledge that supports software engineering is the algorithmic, representational, symbol-processing knowledge of computer science, together with specific knowledge about software and hardware systems.

Symbolic representations are necessary and sufficient for solving information-based problems. Control and data are both represented symbolically. As a result, for example, an analysis program can produce a symbolic description of the path for a machine tool; another program can take this symbolic description as input and produce a symbolic result that is the binary machine code for a cutting tool; and that symbolic representation can be the direct control program for the cutting tool. Notations for symbolic description of control and data enable the definition of software, both the calculations to be performed and the algorithms and data structures. This task is the bread and butter of software implementation, and the existence of symbol strings as a uniform underlying representation of code, data, specification, analysis, and other descriptions simplifies both software design and tool support for software development activities.

Abstraction enables the control of complexity. Abstraction allows the introduction of task-specific concepts and vocabulary, as well as selective control of detail. This in turn allows separation of concerns and a crisp focus on design decisions. A designer of mechanical systems might work with (and expand) a set of abstractions having to do with shapes, weights, and strengths, whereas a designer of accounting systems might work with a set of abstractions having to do with customers, vendors, transactions, inventory, and currency balances. The ability to introduce problem-specific definitions that can, in most respects, be treated as part of the original design language allows software design to be carried out in problem-specific terms, separating the implementation of these abstractions as an independent problem. An additional benefit is that this leads to models and simulations that are selective about the respects in which they are faithful to reality. Some levels of design abstraction, characterized by common phenomena, notations, and concerns, occur repeatedly and independent of underlying technology. The most familiar of these is the programming language, such as Java. The recent emergence of UML has provided a set of diagrammatic[4] design vocabularies that address specific aspects of design, such as the sequence of operations or the allowable transitions between system states. More specialized abstractions are now being used to define "software product families," or design spaces that allow multiple similar software systems to be produced systematically and predictably.

Imposing structure on problems often makes them more tractable, and a number of common structures are available. Designing systems as related sets of independent components allows separation of independent concerns; hierarchy and other relations help explain the relations among the components. In practice, independence is impractical, but software designers can reduce the uncertainty by using well-understood patterns of software organization, called software architectures. An architecture such as a pipe-and filter system, a client-server system, or an application-and-plugin organization provides guidance drawn from prior experience about the kinds of responsibilities to assign to each component and the rules that govern component interaction.

Precise models support analysis and prediction. These models may be formal or empirical. Formal and empirical models are subject to different standards of proof and provide different levels of assurance in their results. For example, a formal model of an interaction protocol can reveal

---

[4]Diagrams are symbolic representations, just as text strings are. The grammars for diagrammatic notations may be more complex than those for textual symbolic representations, but the essential properties are shared.

that implementations will have internal inconsistencies or the possibility of starvation or deadlock. The results support software design by providing predictions of properties of a system early in the system design, when repair is less expensive. Software systems are sufficiently complex that they exhibit emergent properties that do not derive in obvious ways from the properties of the components. Models that support analysis or simulation can reveal these properties early in design, as well.

Engineering Fundamentals

The systematic method and attention to pragmatic solutions that shapes software engineering practice is the practical, goal-directed method of engineering, together with specific knowledge about design and evaluation techniques.

Engineering quality resides in engineering judgment. Tools, techniques, methods, models, and processes are means that support this end. The history of software development is peppered with "methodologies" for designing software and tools for creating and managing code. To the extent that these methods and tools relieve the designer of tedious, error-prone details, they can be very useful. They can enhance sound judgment, and they may make activities more accurate and efficient, but they cannot replace sound judgment and a primary commitment to understanding and satisfying clients' needs.

Engineering requires reconciling conflicting constraints and managing uncertainty. These constraints arise from requirements, from implementation considerations, and from the environment in which the software system will operate. They typically overconstrain the system, so the engineer must find reasonable compromises that reflect the client's priorities. Moreover, the requirements, the available resources, and the operating environment are most often not completely known in advance, and they most often evolve as the software and system are designed. Engineers generate and compare alternative designs, predict the properties of the resulting systems, and choose the most promising alternatives for further refinement and exploration. Finding sufficiently good cost-effective solutions is usually preferable to optimization.

Engineering skills improve as a result of careful systematic reflection on experience. A normal part of any project should be critical evaluation of the work. Critical evaluation of prior and competing work is also important, especially as it informs current design decisions. One of the products of systematic reflection is codified experience, for example in the form of a vocabulary of solution structures and the situations in which they are useful. The designs known as software product lines or software product families define frameworks for collections of related software systems;

these are often created within a company to unify a set of existing products or to guide the development of a next-generation product.

Human, Social, and Economic Fundamentals

The commitment to satisfying clients' needs and managing effective development organizations that guides software engineering business decisions is the organizational and cognitive knowledge about the human and social context, together with specific knowledge about human-computer interaction techniques.

Technology improves exponentially, but human capability does not. The Moore's-law improvements in cost and power of computation (see Hill in Chapter 2) have enabled an unprecedented rate of improvement in technical capability. Unfortunately, the result has often been software products that confuse and frustrate their users rather than providing corresponding improvements in their efficiency or satisfaction. Software developers are increasingly aware of the need to dedicate part of the increase in computing capability to simplifying the use of the more-capable software by adapting systems to the needs of their users.

Cost, time, and business constraints matter, not just capability. Much of computer science focuses on the functionality and performance properties of software, including not only functional correctness but also, for example, speed, reliability, and security. Software engineering must also address other concerns of the client for the software, including the cost of development and ownership, time to delivery, compliance with standards and regulations, contributions to policy objectives, and compatibility with existing software and business processes. These factors affect the system design as well as the project organization.

Software development for practical software-intensive systems usually depends on teamwork by creative people. Both the scale and the diversity of knowledge involved in many modern software applications require the effort and expertise of numerous people. They must combine software design skills and knowledge of the problem domain with business objectives, client needs, and the factors that make creative people effective. As a result, the technical substance of software engineering needs an organizational setting that coordinates their efforts. Software development methods provide guidance about project structure, management procedures, and information structures for tracking the software and related documents.

Software Engineering Research

Software engineering researchers seek better ways to develop practical software, especially software that controls large-scale software-intensive systems that must be highly dependable. They are often motivated by the prospect of affecting the practice of software development, by finding simpler ways to deal with the uncertainties of "wicked problems," and by improving the body of codified or scientific knowledge that can be applied to software development.

Scientific and engineering research fields can be characterized by identifying what they value:

- What kinds of questions are "interesting"?
- What kinds of results help to answer these questions, and what research methods can produce these results?
- What kinds of evidence can demonstrate the validity of a result, and how are good results distinguished from bad ones?

Software engineering research exhibits considerable diversity along these dimensions. Understanding the widely followed research strategies helps explain the character of this research area and the reasons software engineering researchers do the kinds of research that they do.

Physics, biology, and medicine have well-refined public explanations of their research processes. Even in simplified form, these provide guidance about what counts as "good research" both inside and outside the field. For example, the experimental model of physics and the double-blind studies of medicine are understood, at least in broad outline, not only by the research community but also by the public at large. In addition to providing guidance for the design of research in a discipline, these paradigms establish the scope of scientific disciplines through a social and political process of "boundary setting."

Software engineering, however, is still in the process of articulating this sort of commonly understood guidance. One way to identify the common research strategies is to observe the types of research that are accepted in major conferences and journals. These observations here are based specifically on the papers submitted to and accepted by the International Conference on Software Engineering;[5] they are generally representative of the field, though there is some dissonance between research approaches that are advocated publicly and those that are accepted in practice. Another current activity, the Impact Project,[6] seeks to trace the

---

[5]Mary Shaw, 2003, "Writing Good Software Engineering Research Papers," *Proceedings of the 25th International Conference on Software Engineering (ICSE 2003)*, IEEE Computer Society, pp. 726-736.

[6]Impact Project Panel, 2001, "Determining the Impact of Software Engineering Research Upon Practice, Panel Summary," *Proceedings of the 23rd International Conference on Software Engineering (ICSE 2001)*, IEEE Computer Society, p. 697.

influence of software engineering research on practice; the emphasis there is on the dissemination of research rather than the research strategies themselves.

Questions Software Engineering Researchers Care About

Generally speaking, software engineering researchers seek better ways to develop and evaluate software. Development includes all the synthetic activities that involve creating and modifying the software, including the code, design documents, documentation, and so on. Evaluation includes all the analytic activities associated with predicting, determining, and estimating properties of the software systems, including both functionality and extra-functional properties such as performance or reliability.

Software engineering research answers questions about methods of development or analysis, about details of designing or evaluating a particular instance, about generalizations over whole classes of systems or techniques, or about exploratory issues concerning existence or feasibility.

The most common software engineering research seeks an improved method or means of developing software—that is, of designing, implementing, evolving, maintaining, or otherwise operating on the software system itself. Research about methods for reasoning about software systems, principally analysis of correctness (testing and verification), is also fairly common.

Results Software Engineering Researchers Respect

The tangible contributions of software engineering research may be procedures or techniques for development or analysis; they may be models that generalize from specific examples, or they may be specific tools, solutions, or results about particular systems.

By far the most common kind of software engineering research result is a new procedure or technique for development or analysis. Models of various degrees of precision and formality are also common, with better success rates for quantitative than for qualitative models. Tools and notations are well represented, usually as auxiliary results in combination with a procedure or technique.

Evidence Software Engineering Researchers Accept

Software engineers offer several kinds of evidence in support of their research results. It is essential to select a form of validation that is appropriate for the type of research result and the method used to obtain the result. As an obvious example, a formal model should be supported by rigorous derivation and proof, not by one or two simple examples. Yet, a simple example derived from a practical system may play a major role in validating a new type of development method.

The most commonly successful kinds of validation are based on analysis and real-world experience. Well-chosen examples are also successful.

Additional Observations

As in other areas of computer science, maturation of software engineering as a research area has brought more focused, and increasingly explicit, expectations for the quality of research—care in framing questions, quality of evidence, reasoning behind conclusions.

Software engineering remains committed to developing ways to create useful solutions to practical problems. This commitment to dealing with the real world, warts and all, means that software engineering researchers will often have to contend with impure data and under-controlled observations. Most computer science researchers aspire to results that are both theoretically well grounded and practical. Unfortunately, practical problems often require either the simplification of the problem in order to achieve theoretically sound conclusions or else the sacrifice of certainty in the results in favor of results that address the practical aspects of the problem. Software engineering researchers tend to choose the latter course more often than the former.

The community of computer users seems to have a boundless appetite for information-processing capability. Fueled by our collective imagination, this appetite seems to grow even faster than Moore's-law technology growth. This demand for larger scale and complexity, coupled with an increasing emphasis on dependability and ease of use—especially for users with little computer training—generates new problems, and even new classes of problems for software engineering.

8

Research Behind
Everyday Computation

Computer science research has led to the emergence of entirely new capabilities used by millions of ordinary people today. Using computers to typeset text was probably foreseeable, but the ease with which anyone can become a small-scale publisher by using the Web was harder to envision. Automating accountants' ledger paper was perhaps natural, but the ability to disintermediate the financial-analysis function—moving control from a central data-processing department to a spreadsheet on an executive's desk—could not have been. Creating an index of documents stored at various Internet locations so that they could be shared by a community of physics researchers was, perhaps, not astounding, but leveraging the power of distributed access, the universal name-space of the uniform resource locator (URL), and easily usable browsers together with new algorithms for searching has led to an explosion of information-retrieval opportunities that has changed forever the way we do business.

Computers now perform most of the document-preparation tasks that used to be handled by secretaries: typing drafts, correcting drafts, positioning figures, formatting final copy, and the like. Ullman traces the 30-year evolution of text-formatting programs from quick-and-dirty typesetters created by graduate students to avoid typing their theses to the powerful document-formatters of the present day.

Similarly, Foley shows how today's spreadsheets, which began as a program to help accountants manage ledger sheets, astonished the computer-science world by becoming the "killer application" that transferred effective control of computing to non-programmers in all disciplines.

One of the principal personal uses of computers today is searching the Internet's wealth of online information. The idea of information retrieval is far from new, but the ability to dedicate computing power to amplifying human effort has led to new wrinkles, such as attempts to establish the relevance of information based on the number of people referring to it. Norvig explains the technology behind modern Internet searches.

HOW YOU GOT MICROSOFT WORD

Jeffrey Ullman, Stanford University and Gradience Corporation

Those born after about 1975 cannot imagine the cumbersome process by which formal documents, ranging from business letters to books, were produced. Drafts were hand-written and then typed by a secretary using a typewriter. If corrections were needed, small errors could be handled by erasing or by applying whiteout, followed by typing of the correct words. But length-changing errors required that the entire page be retyped and the error-checking process be repeated. When computers first became widespread in businesses and schools, many people started typing their documents on punch cards. Similar to the cards that were used in the famous Florida vote of 2000, the cards represent letters when you punch out certain holes, creating "chad."

A document such as a thesis could be typed on cards, fed to the computer, and printed line-for-line on a printer. Early printers were like typewriters, but faster. This arrangement solved the problem of handling small errors, since only one or a few cards would have to be repunched. Several early computer-science students saw the potential for doing better, especially as they confronted the daunting task of typing their PhD theses. In 1964, Jerry Saltzer at the Massachusetts Institute of Technology created for this purpose a pair of programs: Typeset, which was an early form of a text editor, and Runoff, which was an improved formatting system. Bob Balzer, at Carnegie Mellon University, created software similar to Runoff, called LEAD (List, Edit, and Display), at about the same time. Programs like Runoff and LEAD not only reproduced what was on punch cards, but also formatted the document by placing on one line as many words as would fit, typically a maximum of 80 characters per line. This advance solved the problem of having to retype large amounts of text when words were inserted or deleted. Special commands, which were not part of the text, could be inserted to control matters such as justification, that is, alignment of text on the right, as in a book, as well as on the left.

Word-Processing Software at Bell Labs

The Typeset/Runoff system inspired a group of researchers at Bell Laboratories, leading to Joe Ossanna's NROFF (new runoff) program. A "macro" capability was added to allow repetitive formatting concepts, such as section headers or indented paragraphs, to be defined once and used easily many times. The "MS" macro package by Mike Lesk was widely used as a standard for formatting of text. But the printed output device was still a souped-up typewriter, with its single size and font of letters.

In the early 1970s, work on typesetting at Bell Labs had progressed to the point where the labs purchased a CAT phototypesetting machine, of the kind used at the time to produce newspapers, for example. This device allowed printing to be done in several fonts and font sizes. Unlike today's laser printers, it printed only on photographic paper, which was then reproduced by one of several processes, such as a "Xerox machine." NROFF evolved into TROFF (typesetter runoff) to allow documents to be created that were then typeset on film. For the first time, it became possible for casual authors to produce a letter or report that looked as if it were part of a book.

However, TROFF was not up to the requirement faced by many scientists and engineers to set mathematical text easily. While the CAT printer could, for example, print a subscript in the correct (smaller) size and below the line of text, there was no convenient way to tell it to do so. EQN, a program written by Brian Kernighan, solved that problem by taking expressions that represented how the equation or formula should look (e.g., "X sub 1" for an X with a subscript 1, X_1) and turning them into TROFF, while leaving everything that wasn't equations intact, for later processing by TROFF. EQN is in effect an atypical programming language, since it does not let you write general-purpose algorithms, as the best-known programming languages do, but it helps you deal with a particular, difficult problem, that of describing how mathematical expressions should look on the page. It is an excellent example of how the effective design of a language or notation for a problem leads to tools that people find useful and powerful. A key borrowing of EQN from the more traditional programming languages is recursion, one of the central themes of computing, where things are defined partially in terms of themselves. For example, EQN allows one to say not only "X sub 1" but "X sub anything" or even "anything sub anything," where the "anythings" can themselves have subscripts or any of the other operations whereby mathematical expressions are built up, such as by horizontal lines for division. Thus, one can say things like "X sub {n sub i} " to represent an X whose subscript is itself a subscripted "n sub i" (x_{n_i}).

Several other components of modern word processors got their start in the same Bell Labs group. The first spell-checkers were developed to compare words in the document with a list of "acceptable" words, modified by rules for plurals, tense modifications, and so on. Also, Lorinda Cherry developed the first grammar-checker (DICT, for "diction") by applying a table of rules to the document.

Typesetting Research at Xerox PARC

In the mid-1970s, a team of researchers at Xerox PARC (Palo Alto Research Center) made several important contributions toward the way we now create documents. One was the development of the laser printer. While the Xerox PARC researchers could and did build a laser printer, they could not do so at a price people would pay. They estimated that it would cost over $100,000 at that time for the printer we now buy for a few hundred dollars. Nevertheless, in order to verify their conjecture that the existence of these devices would change the way people dealt with documents, they built prototypes of a laser printer, called Dover, and gave them to several universities. As envisioned, the Dover changed markedly the way students and faculty prepared papers. Also as envisioned, the cost for building such devices has dropped dramatically over the years, and the dream of a laser printer on every desk has become real.

A second innovation from the PARC group was the WYSIWYG (wizzy-wig, or "what you see is what you get") editor. A prototype text editor called Bravo allowed users to see the document they were creating. In one sense, the differences between Bravo and TROFF were small. For example, each allowed you to specify that certain text should be italics. In Bravo, as in MSWord and other text-processing systems today, one could change fonts, say to italics, as one typed. In contrast, TROFF required you to type a command (".it") to say "change to italics." Bravo allowed you to see that you were really typing italic text (and would also let you see if you forgot to return to roman text when you should), while with TROFF, you could only tell whether you got it right when you printed your document later. On the other hand, Bravo was less adept at setting complex mathematical formulas, since it did not possess the recursive description capabilities of EQN, and in fact, the successors of Bravo up to this day have not recaptured the power of EQN in WYSIWYG mode. While it may seem obvious that for non-mathematical typesetting, WYSIWYG editors are a wonderful tool, the existence of such editors depends on developments in a number of different areas. Of course, processors had to become fast enough that it became economical to devote a processor to a single task like editing. Computer graphics technology needed to advance to a state where it was possible to offer the user a video terminal as a display unit. Operating systems needed to incorporate windows as a primitive concept and manage rapid communication and drawing of characters, between keyboard, processor, and display.

The TeX Project

At about the same time as the Xerox activities, Don Knuth at Stanford began a broad study of how computers can improve the preparation and typesetting of documents. By this time, it was clear that the font was a critical computer object. Descriptions of the letters in a font have to be developed so the same look can be displayed on a video terminal and also printed, perhaps at a different size, on one of many different printing devices. For this purpose, Knuth developed a system called Metafont for describing the shapes of letters and other characters in a way that allows easy generation of the font in different sizes and slants. Knuth also developed TeX, a unified system for typesetting that incorporates the capabilities of TROFF and several specialized systems such as EQN. In addition, TeX increases the care with which paragraphs and pages are laid out. TeX's paragraphing algorithm looks at the words of an entire paragraph before deciding on line-breaks, and thereby improves the look of the text when compared with "greedy" algorithms that look at text a line at a time and fit whatever they can on each line in succession. The TeX paragraphing algorithm is an excellent example of a general computational approach called "dynamic programming." It works roughly as follows. First, we need a measure of how well words fit on a line. A typical approach, even for greedy algorithms, is to decide on the optimum space between words and then assign a "badness" to a line proportional to the square of the deviations of the spaces from the optimal. The objective then becomes to minimize the total badness of all the lines in a paragraph.

Now the number of ways to break a paragraph of, say, 100 words into 10 lines is astronomical; it is the number of ways to pick 9 line breaks among the 99 positions between the words, which is "99 choose 9," or about 1.7 trillion. It is clearly not feasible to consider all possible ways to break paragraphs. Fortunately, as is often the case in computer science, the obvious way to do something is neither the best way nor the only way. In this case, dynamic programming let Knuth find an algorithm that takes time proportional to the length of the paragraph, rather than to some exponential in the size of the paragraph.

The dynamic programming algorithm fills out a table of least badnesses, not just for the paragraph itself, but for all paragraphs that could be formed from a tail or suffix of the sequence of words in the paragraph. That is, for each i, starting at 1 and going up to the number of words in the paragraph, the entry for i is the least badness of any division of the last i words into lines. Suppose we have computed this value for 1, 2, . . . up to $i-1$. To decide on the best line breaks for the last i words, we consider, for all k small enough that k words can fit on one line, the cost of placing the first k of the i words on one line (using the formula for the "badness" of any particular line), plus the badness of the best breaking for the remaining $i - k$ words (as given by the table). As soon as i reaches the total number of words in the paragraph, we know the cost of the best line breaking, and we can easily figure out what that breaking is, by storing in the table, as we go, the winning value of k for each i.

In addition, one of Knuth's students, Frank Liang, invented an elegant algorithm for choosing the points at which words should be hyphenated. The dictionary tells us how to hyphenate in a straghtforward way: it lists every word it knows and shows where the hyphens may go. In addition to using a lot of space, that approach is of little use if you've just invented a word like "cyberpunk," or you need to hyphenate a proper noun. Liang's approach was to summarize the rules of hyphenation, using a simple language for expressing those rules and their priorities.

Imagine a collection of rules—it's good to hyphenate here; it's not good to hyphenate there. For instance, it is generally a bad idea to hyphenate between the "a" and "t" in ". . . at . . . ." But if the word happens to fit the pattern ". . . ation . . .," then it is actually a good idea to hyphenate between the "a" and "t" if the word has to be hyphenated. Each rule has a number associated with it, and this number is given to those points between letters to which the rule applies. Thus, a point might acquire several different numbers, from different rules. If so, take the largest of the numbers and ignore the rest. The magic of Liang's algorithm is this: if the number associated with a point is odd, then you may hyphenate there; if it is even, you may not. For example, the rule about ". . . at . . ." might receive a low, even number, like 2. That number suggests that in the absence of any more specific pattern, let's not hyphenate here. The rule about ". . . ation . . .," on the other hand, would have a high, odd number, such as 9. Thus, the rule strongly suggests "a-tion" is a good hyphenation, and overrules the more general idea that "a-t" is bad. Were we to have a specific word in mind with pattern ". . . ation . . ." where we did not want the hyphen between the "a" and "t" (there are no such examples in common English), we could make that word a pattern with a still higher, even number, like 24.

Word Processing Today

If you are familiar with MSWord or a similar application such as WordPerfect, you will know that many of the ideas described here are available to you. The application breaks paragraphs into lines in a way that allows alignment at both left and right (although it does not use the TeX algorithm for doing so). It allows changes of font at the press of a button on the screen. It allows global changes in the way elements such as sections are displayed, just as the early Bell Labs macro packages did. It has a rule-based system to catch many grammatical errors, like DICT did, and catches spelling errors in a similar way. It has a WYSIWYG interface like the old Bravo editor, and it easily passes its document to a laser printer, a descendant of the Dover printers of 25 years ago. The system provides a virtually unlimited number of fonts.

Perhaps as a reflection on how prevalent word processing has become in ordinary discourse, neither Microsoft nor other manufacturers of word-processing applications have felt the need to integrate mathematical type-setting nearly as closely as did EQN. Ironically, many scientists and engineers still prefer to write using TeX (which has all the power of EQN and more), or its variant LaTeX, a system developed by Leslie Lamport.

VISICALC, SPREADSHEETS, AND PROGRAMMING FOR THE MASSES, OR "HOW A KILLER APP WAS BORN"

James D. Foley, Georgia Institute of Technology

An important part of computing is the study of human computer interaction—HCI. Individuals and organizations generally buy computer hardware and software expecting that the computer will allow them to do something entirely new, or more accurately or completely or quickly or economically or with more enjoyment than without the computer. The role of HCI is to develop computer capabilities that match what people want to do, so that the computer can be useful to individuals and organizations.[1]

At least three important software innovations in the last 30 years have been HCI tours de force:

• The development of window managers at SRI and PARC, which were precursors to the Macintosh and Microsoft window manager software that allowed millions of people to easily use personal computers.

• The development of the first Web browser by Tim Berners-Lee in 1991;[2] the development of Mosaic (the first widely available browser) at the University of Illinois in 1993, and their subsequent progeny Netscape Navigator and Internet Explorer, which made the World Wide Web accessible to millions of people as opposed to the thousands who had been using it originally.

• VisiCalc, developed by Dan Bricklin and Bob Frankston in 1979. Prior to VisiCalc, personal computers were bought mostly by hobbyists, game players, and to teach programming. The VisiCalc spreadsheet program (whose commercial successors include Microsoft's Excel) caused many financial analysts, business people, accountants, and students to buy personal computers (first the Apple II and later the IBM PC). As such, VisiCalc was the "killer app" that dramatically increased sales of these computers.

VisiCalc

In this essay we focus on VisiCalc, for several reasons. First, VisiCalc did spark the sales of personal computers. Second, VisiCalc introduced

---

[1]See, for example, Brad A. Myers, 1998, "A Brief History of Human Computer Interaction Technology," *ACM Interactions* 5(2):44-54. Available online at http://www-2.cs.cmu.edu/ ~ mulet/papers/uihistory.tr.html.

[2]See http://www.w3.org/History.html.

many of its users to computer programming without their ever realizing they were doing computer programming, thereby providing a powerful tool in an easy-to-use package. And finally, as with window managers and Mosaic, VisiCalc could not have happened without a considerable body of prior computer science research.

Why did VisiCalc spark PC sales? Why did people rush to buy a computer in order to use VisiCalc? Simply because VisiCalc met a market need (a human need) to organize and calculate numbers more rapidly using an electronic spreadsheet than one could do by hand with a paper-based spreadsheet and an adding machine or an electronic calculator. There was a pent-up demand, and VisiCalc together with the PC met that demand. As time went on, other uses for VisiCalc developed—many of us organize lists of address and other information in the convenient row and column format of our favorite spreadsheet, perhaps never calculating a single number. These uses may not have been what Bricklin and Frankston envisioned, but are typical of the way in which tools are adapted by their users to meet needs not envisioned by the tools' designers.

What about this notion that VisiCalc users are actually programming? Well, the "equations" of VisiCalc, by which one states that a particular cell of the spreadsheet is to have a value computed from other cells, are essentially the same as the assignment statements and expressions used in all modern programming languages. The VisiCalc equation "= (B6 + B7)/(C4 + C5) – D9" placed in cell B9 has the same effect[3] as the C programming language statement B9 = (B6 + B7)/(C4 + C5) – D9 or the Pascal statement "B9 := (B6 + B7)/(C4 + C5) – D9" or the Java statement "B9 = (B6 + B7)/(C4 + C5) – D9." But, referring back to the concept of the universal machine (see Kleinberg and Papadimitriou in Chapter 2), it is not the case that this limited form of programming in VisiCalc is the equivalent of a general programming capability.

VisiCalc allowed and encouraged its users to program without realizing that they were programming, using the simple-to-understand formulae that could either be typed into a spreadsheet cell or be partially or in some cases completely entered simply by pointing to the cells in the spreadsheet that appear in the equation. Hence, a reduction in the "fear of programming" that often discouraged people from putting computers to use.

How did VisiCalc draw on computer science research? In multiple ways:

---

[3]Strictly speaking, as soon as any of the variables such as B6 or C5 change, the equation is re-evaluated and the new value is placed in cell B9, whereas with the programming languages the assignment statement is executed only when the program flow of control comes to the statement. This means that the VisiCalc equation is a more powerful construct than the programming language assignment statement.

1. By using a visual "what you see is what you get" (WYSIWYG) user interface, in which one sees the spreadsheet and can directly manipulate cells in the spreadsheet by pointing at them.

Dan Bricklin states in his Web pages[4] that he was aware of and influenced by the early research work of Doug Engelbart on text editors using a mouse, and that he had probably seen a demonstration of Xerox PARC's Alto computer system, which was in turn also influenced by Engelbart. Engelbart and PARC are the critical early developers of the key elements of contemporary window-oriented user interfaces found in the Macintosh and Microsoft operating systems.

Engelbart's passion was to augment the human intellect by providing computer tools to help organize information, compose and modify documents, and work with others at a distance while doing this. With this vision, he and a group (up to 17 researchers) developed NLS (oN-Line System) between 1962 and 1969 at the Stanford Research Institute.

Along the way, they invented the mouse as a way to interact with the computer by pointing rather than by the much slower process of moving a cursor with key strokes; developed tiled windows (non-overlapping, as opposed to the overlapping windows of Microsoft Windows and the Apple Macintosh operating system); developed a text editor with commands to move, copy, and delete individual characters, words, or blocks of text (see Ullman in Chapter 8); and provided hyperlinks (just like in the World Wide Web) and key-word searches (similar to the search-engine concept of Google and Alta Vista).

Englebart's research style is not unusual; set a big, hard-to-achieve goal, and create multiple tools needed to achieve that goal. The same thing happened at Xerox PARC. The Alto workstation software developed at PARC starting in the early 1970s was the prototype for the Apple Macintosh and Microsoft Windows user interfaces. Alto had many of the features seen in these and other contemporary window interfaces: windows, icons, menus, copy and paste commands, and direct-manipulation text and graphics editors.

2. By using "programming by example" to simplify and speed up the process of entering equations.

VisiCalc was the first widely used instance of "programming by example," in which the user does programming by demonstrating operations to the computer rather than by specifying what is to be done via

---

[4]See http://www.bricklin.com/visicalc.htm.

some programming language. For example, to indicate that a cell should always have in it the sum of several other cells, one would point at the cell that has the sum, and then successively to the cells that are to be summed.

The idea of programming by example was developed in a slightly different form by Moshe Zloof of IBM research a few years earlier. Zloof wanted to allow users to specify database queries without having to learn a query programming language (such as SQL). His insight was to recognize that if a user gave just an example of the query results such as a list of part numbers, descriptions, inventory quantity, and selling price, then the query language statement(s) to obtain all of the results could be generated from the example.

VisiCalc applied the concept in a slightly different way than did Zloof, thus both drawing on and contributing to the storehouse of computer science knowledge (a typical pattern for CS and other research). Specifically, VisiCalc allows the user to enter a formula (such as given above) by pointing at the cells that occur in the formula. So to enter the formula B2 + C5 in cell B1, the user points at cell B1, types = to indicate that a formula is being specified, then points at cell B2, then points at cell C5, and ends by typing the enter key. The + in the formula is assumed and entered automatically, as the most common choice. If the product is desired rather than the sum, the user types "*"after pointing at cell B2 and before pointing at cell C5.

This seemingly simple idea greatly simplifies the process of entering formulae, and it corresponds nicely to the intuition that, given a choice between pointing at something and typing the name of something (in the case at hand, the spreadsheet cell), we humans will tend to point rather than name, as the easier of the two alternatives.

3. By applying finite state machine notation as a tool for designing the program—what inputs were valid in each "state," what response the computer would make to each input, and what new program "state" would result.

The understanding of how to use state diagrams for specifying the behavior of interactive programs was first developed by William Newman in 1968 as a researcher at Imperial College, London. He, in turn, drew on the fundamental notion of finite state machines that had been developed as yet another computer science concept. The idea as applied to VisiCalc is that the program can be in one of a finite number of states. In each state, only certain user actions (such as entering information into a cell, or selecting a command) are possible. Each such action takes the program to another state (or back to the same state) and at the same time causes some change in what the user sees on the display.

4. By using language parsing techniques.

Computer scientists have developed techniques for taking expressions such as the earlier example of the expression (B6 + B7)/(C4 + C5) – D9 stored in cell B9 and actually performing the calculations in the appropriate sequence. With the example expression, the actual sequence of arithmetic operations would be:

> Add cells B6 and B7, saving the result in a place called TEMP1.
> Add cells C4 and C5, saving the result in a place called TEMP2.
> Add TEMP1 and TEMP2, saving the results in TEMP1.
> Add TEMP1 and cell D9, saving the results in cell B9.

This may seem simple, but try writing out a general procedure that will work with an arbitrary expression, with many parentheses and divisions and multiplications! Not so easy, is it?

The Next "Killer App"

What will be the successor to VisiCalc, to windowing systems, to Web browsers that will provide new capabilities to millions and tens of millions of computer users? There are many possibilities; I believe that whatever the next major development, the next "killer app," might be, it will:

- Meet an individual or organizational need.
- Draw on the research of many, many computer scientists.
- Leverage the existing hardware and software infrastructure, and accelerate their growth (just) as VisiCalc leveraged and accelerated the availability of PCs and e-mail leveraged the Internet and Web browsers leveraged the World Wide Web protocols.

We also note that only Web browsing was well anticipated as a killer app—anticipated by Vannevar Bush in the 1940s and researched by a number of prominent computer scientists from the late 1960s into the 1980s.

Many candidates for the next "killer app" recognize that the now-common use of computers by people sitting at a desk may not be the major way of using computers in the future. A fundamentally new direction for computing is evolving: I call this direction off-the-desk-top computing, in the sense that it will not be desk-top computers but other forms of computers that will create the next revolution. Others call it ubiquitous or embedded computing, in the sense that computing will be everywhere (i.e., ubiquitous) and embedded in all manner of devices and equipment. This is already happening. Contemporary cell phones have a computer that is as powerful as desk-top computers of 10 years ago. TV set-top boxes have as much computing power as powerful engineering workstations of 5 years ago. The typical automobile has 10 to 20 computers with aggregate power comparable to a contemporary desk-top PC.

The most widespread hardware and software infrastructure that might be leveraged is the wireless phone system. It is already pervasive, and it is computer intensive. It is already heavily used for short text messages, for games, and to obtain information. And, with the small size of wireless phones and their keypads, and the integration of wireless functionality into personal digital assistants and with the clear benefit of voice recognition in using small devices, a trend can surely be predicted. More generally, voice recognition will become more and more pervasive as algorithms improve and as computing power and memory become ever more available.

Another hardware and software infrastructure that will be leveraged is the World Wide Web itself. With vast amounts of information online and more and more of the world citizenry connected, the use of intelligent assistants to find information, to make sense of information, and to use information will surely expand. Current examples include comparison shopping, money management, and travel arrangements. Life has become more complex and fast-moving; perhaps computers can help simplify life in some ways.

Automobiles already have dozens of computers, many networked together. They serve just one of two purposes—operating the car, or entertaining/communicating with the driver and passengers. Many cars already have built-in wireless phones, global positioning systems, limited voice recognition, and navigation aids. Many people spend tens of hours a week in a car, and there are significant personal and societal benefits to further leveraging the automotive computing infrastructure to make driving safer, to connect us with the outside world, and to entertain us.

We spend significant amounts of time at home. Many predictions are made for computer-based home entertainment systems and the broader "wired home," but the home has a very weak hardware and software infrastructure—nothing like that of the car or the typical office working environment or the wireless phone. I believe that homes will ultimately have networked appliances, switches, lights, motion sensors, cameras, microphones, and so on. While we do not yet have a killer app, we have candidates such as the use of computers to allow older people to live alone at home for more years before having to live with their children or in a nursing home; energy management; and home security.

We should not neglect new uses of the Internet and the Web. Amy Bruckman, in her essay in Chapter 7, nicely likens our use of the Web to the early days when the automobile was still known as the "horseless buggy." At that time, nearly a century ago, one could not imagine the cars and highways of today.

While we can and should be proactive in exploring these possibilities and their implications for our lives, it is also true that only time will tell.

INTERNET SEARCHING

Peter Norvig, Google Inc.

In 300 BC, the Library of Alexandria held some half million scrolls and served as a cultural center for the world, uniting the thoughts of Greek, Egyptian, Macedonian, and Babylonian culture. According to the *Letter of Aristeas*, the library had "a large budget in order to collect, if possible, all the books in the world." Whole fields of study such as geometry and grammar grew from the scholars who had the fortune to travel to and study at Alexandria.

In 2004 AD, the Internet forms a distributed library of billions of pages, one that is accessible to anyone, anywhere in the world, at the click of a mouse. Every day hundreds of millions of "trips" to the library start with a query to an Internet search engine. If I want to research a topic such as "Library of Alexandria," I can type those words to a search engine and in less than a second have access to a list of 31,000 pages, sorted by their usefulness to the query. This unprecedented ease of access to information has revolutionized the way research is done by students, scientists, journalists, shoppers, and others. It opens up an online marketplace of products, services, and ideas that benefits both information providers and seekers; sellers and buyers; consumers and advertisers.

How is it that an Internet search engine can find the answers to a query so quickly? It is a four-step process:

1. *Crawling* the Web, following links to find pages;
2. *Indexing* the pages to create an index from every word to every place it occurs;
3. *Ranking* the pages so the best ones show up first; and
4. *Displaying* the results in a way that is easy for the user to understand.

Crawling is conceptually quite simple: starting at some well-known sites on the Web, recursively follow every hypertext link, recording the pages encountered along the way. In computer science this is called the transitive closure of the *link* relation. However, the conceptual simplicity hides a large number of practical complications: sites may be busy or down at one point and come back to life later; pages may be duplicated at multiple sites (or with different URLs at the same site) and must be dealt with accordingly; many pages have text that does not conform to the standards for HTML, HTTP redirection, robot exclusion, or other protocols; some information is hard to access because it is hidden behind a form, Flash animation, or Javascript program. Finally, the necessity of crawling 100 million pages a day means that building a crawler is an exercise in distributed computing, requiring many computers that must work together and schedule their actions so as to get to all the pages without overwhelming any one site with too many requests at once.

A search engine's *index* is similar to the index in the back of a book: it is used to find the pages on which a word occurs. There are two main differences: the search engine's index lists every occurrence of every word, not just the important concepts, and the number of pages is in the billions, not hundreds. Various techniques of compression and clever representation are used to keep the index "small," but it is still measured in terabytes (millions of megabytes), which again means that distributed computing is required. Most modern search engines index *link* data as well as word data. It is useful to know how many pages link to a given page, and what the quality of those pages is. This kind of analysis is similar to citation analysis in bibliographic work and helps establish which pages are authoritative. Algorithms such as PageRank and HITS are used to assign a numeric measure of authority to each page. For example, the PageRank algorithm says that the rank of a page is a function of the sum of the ranks of the pages that link to the page. If we let PR(p) be the PageRank of page p, Out(p) be the number of outgoing links from page p, Links(p) be the set of pages that link to page p, and N be the total number of pages in the index, then we can define PageRank by

$$PR(p) = r \: / \: N + (1 - r) \sum\nolimits_{i \subset Links(p)} PR(i) \: / \: Out(i)$$

where r is a parameter that indicates the probability that a user will choose not to follow a link, but will instead restart at some other page. The r/N term means that each of the N pages is equally likely to be the restart point, although it is also possible to use a smaller subset of well-known pages as the restart candidates. Note that the formula for PageRank is recursive—PR appears on both the right- and left-hand sides of the equation. The equation can be solved by iterating several times, or by employing algorithms that compute the eigenvalues of a (4-billion-by-4-billion) matrix.

The two steps above are *query independent*—they do not depend on the user's query and thus can be done before a query is issued, with the cost shared among all users. This is why a search takes a second or less, rather than the days it would take if a search engine had to crawl the Web anew for each query. We now consider what happens when a user types a query.

Consider the query ["National Academies" computer science], where the square brackets denote the beginning and end of the query, and the quotation marks indicate that the enclosed words must be found as an exact phrase match. The first step in responding to this query is to look in the index for the *hit lists* corresponding to each of the four words "National," "Academies," "computer," and "science." These four lists are then intersected to yield the set of pages that mention all four words. Because "National Academies" was entered as a phrase, only hits where these two words appear adjacent and in that order are counted. The result is a list of 19,000 or so pages.

The next step is *ranking* these 19,000 pages to decide which ones are most relevant. In traditional information retrieval this is done by counting the number of occurrences of each word, weighing rare words more heavily than frequent words, and normalizing for the length of the page. A number of refinements on this scheme have been developed, so it is common to give more credit for pages where the words occur near each other, where the words are in bold or large font, or in a title, or where the words occur in the anchor text of a link that points to the page. In addition the query-independent authority of each page is factored in. The result is a numeric score for each page that can be used to sort them best-first. For our four-word query, most search engines agree that the Computer Science and Telecommunications Board home page at www7.nationalacademies.org/cstb/ is the best result, although one preferred the National Academies news page at www.nas.edu/topnews/ and one inexplicably chose a year-old news story that mentioned the Academies.

The final step is *displaying* the results. Traditionally this is done by listing a short description of each result in rank-sorted order. The description will include the title of the page and may include additional information such as a short abstract or excerpt from the page. Some search engines generate query-independent abstracts while others customize each excerpt to show at least some of the words from the query. Displaying this kind of query-dependent excerpt means that the search engine must keep a copy of the full text of the pages (in addition to the index) at a cost of several more terabytes. Some search engines attempt to cluster the result pages into coherent categories or folders, although this technology is not yet mature.

Studies have shown that the most popular uses of computers are e-mail, word processing, and Internet searching. Of the three, Internet searching is by far the most sophisticated example of computer science technology. Building a high-quality search engine requires extensive knowledge and experience in information retrieval, data structure design, user interfaces, and distributed systems implementation.

Future advances in searching will increasingly depend on statistical natural-language processing (see Lee in Chapter 6) and machine-learning (see Mitchell in Chapter 6) techniques. With so much data—billions of pages, tens of billions of links, and hundreds of millions of queries per day—it makes sense to use data-mining approaches to automatically improve the system. For example, several search engines now do spelling correction of user queries. It turns out that the vast amount of correctly and incorrectly spelled text available to a search engine makes it easier to create a good spelling corrector than traditional techniques based on dictionaries. It is likely that there will be other examples of text understanding that can be accomplished better with a data-oriented approach; this is an area that search engines are just beginning to explore.

Recommended Reading

Chakrabarti, S., B. Dom, D. Gibson, J. Kleinberg, S.R. Kumar, P. Raghavan, S. Rajagopalan, and A. Tomkins, 1999, "Hypersearching the Web," *Scientific American*, June, pp. 54-60.

9

Personal Statements of Passion About Computer Science Research

W e close with some reflections by computer scientists on the nature of the field and the sources of their passion in their own work.

Sussman identifies a distinctive characteristic of computer science as "procedural epistemology"—the representation of imperative knowledge that allows us to treat a symbolic expression as data for purposes of analysis and as procedure for purposes of dynamic interpretation. The ability to represent data and procedures in symbolic form provides the enormous power of precise expression and reasoning.

Newell writing in 1976 is enchanted by the notion that computer technology may incorporate intelligent behavior into objects. We can create "frozen action to be thawed when needed," and the action can be conditional on the state of the world.

We close with one of the oldest attempts among computer scientists to define computer science. In a reprinted letter first published in 1967, Newell, Perlis, and Simon characterize computer science broadly as the study of the phenomena surrounding computers.

THE LEGACY OF COMPUTER SCIENCE

Gerald Jay Sussman, Massachusetts Institute of Technology

We have witnessed and participated in great advances, in transportation, in computation, in communication, and in biotechnology. But the advances that look like giant steps to us will pale into insignificance by contrast with the even bigger steps in the future. Sometimes I try to imagine what we, the technologists of the second half of the 20th century, will be remembered for, if anything, hundreds of years from now.

In the distant past there were people who lived on the banks of the Nile River. Each year the Nile overflowed its banks, wiping out land boundaries but providing fertile soil for growing crops. As a matter of economic necessity the Egyptians invented ways of surveying the land. They also invented ways of measuring time, to help predict the yearly deluge. Similar discoveries were made in many places in the world. Holders of this practical knowledge were held in high esteem, and the knowledge was transferred to future generations through secret cults. These early surveyors laid the foundation for the development of geometry ("earth measurement" in Greek) by Pythagoras and Euclid and their colleagues around 350 BC. Geometry is a precise language for talking about space. It can be taught to children. (Euclid's *Elements* has been used in this way for more than 2000 years.) It makes the children smarter, by giving them ways of expressing knowledge about arrangements in space and time. It is because of these Greeks that we can tell a child, "If you build it out of triangles it will not collapse the way it does when you build it out of rectangles."

The Rhind Papyrus from Egypt (c. 1650 BC) is the earliest document that we have that discusses what we now think of as algebra problems. Diophantus, another Greek, wrote a book about these ideas in the third century A.D. Algebra was further developed by Abu Abd-Allah ibn Musa Al-Khwarizmi (c. 780–c. 850) and others. (Note: "algebra" = al'jabr is an Arabic word meaning "the recombining of broken parts.") Algebra is also a precise language that gives us the ability to express knowledge about the relationships among quantities, and to make deductions from that knowledge, without necessarily knowing the values of those quantities.

For a long time people were able to predict the motions of some of the heavenly bodies using ad hoc theories derived from observation and philosophical considerations. Claudius Ptolemy wrote the *Almagest*, a famous compendium of this knowledge, in the second century. About 350 years ago Descartes, Galileo, Newton, Leibnitz, Euler, and their contemporaries turned mechanics into a formal science. In the process they invented continuous variables, coordinate geometry, and calculus. We now can talk about motion precisely. This achievement gives us the words to say such sentences as, "When the car struck the tree it was going 50 km/hour." Now every child can understand this sentence and know what is meant by it.

In each of these cases there was an advance in human intelligence, ultimately available to ordinary children, that was precipitated by an advance in mathematics, the precise means of expression. Such advances are preceded by a long history of informal development of practical technique. We are now in the midst of an intellectual revolution that promises to have as much impact on human culture as the cases I have just described.

We have been programming universal computers for about 50 years. The practice of computation arose from military, scientific, business, and accounting applications. Just as the early Egyptian surveyors probably thought of themselves as experts in the development and application of surveying instruments, so have we developed a priestly cult of "computer scientists." But, as I have pointed out (H. Abelson, G.J. Sussman, and J. Sussman, *Structure and Interpretation of Computer Programs*, 2nd Edition, MIT Press, Cambridge, Mass., 1996):

> Computer Science is not a science, and its ultimate significance has little to do with computers. The computer revolution is a revolution in the way we think and in the way we express what we think. The essence of this change is the emergence of what might best be called *procedural epistemology*—the study of the structure of knowledge from an imperative point of view, as opposed to the more declarative point of view taken by classical mathematical subjects. Traditional mathematics provides a framework for dealing precisely with notions of "what is." Computation provides a framework for dealing precisely with notions of "how to."

Computation provides us with new tools to express ourselves. This has already had an impact on the way we teach other engineering subjects. For example, one often hears a student or teacher complain that the student knows the "theory" of the material but cannot effectively solve problems. We should not be surprised: the student has no formal way to learn technique. We expect the student to learn to solve problems by an inefficient process: the student watches the teacher solve a few problems, hoping to abstract the general procedures from the teacher's behavior with particular examples. The student is never given any instructions on how to abstract from examples, nor is the student given any language for expressing what has been learned. It is hard to learn what one cannot express.

In particular, in an introductory subject on electrical circuits we show students the mathematical descriptions of the behaviors of idealized circuit elements such as resistors, capacitors, inductors, diodes, and transistors. We also show them the formulation of Kirchoff's laws, which describe the behaviors of interconnections. From these facts it is possible, in principle, to deduce the behavior of an interconnected combination of components. However, it is not easy to teach the techniques of circuit analysis. The problem is that for most interesting circuits there are many equations and the equations are quite complicated. So it takes organizational skills and judgment to effectively formulate the useful equations and to deduce the interesting behaviors from those equations.

Traditionally, we try to communicate these skills by carefully solving selected problems on a blackboard, explaining our reasoning and organization. We hope that the students can learn by emulation, from our examples. However, the process of induction of a general plan from specific examples does not work very well, so it takes many examples and much hard work on the part of the faculty and students to transfer the skills.

However, if I can assume that my students are literate in a computer programming language, then I can use programs to communicate ideas about *how to* solve problems: I can write programs that describe the general technique of solving a class of problems and give that program to the students to read. Such a program is precise and unambiguous—it can be executed by a dumb computer! In a nicely designed computer language a well-written program can be read by students, who will then have a precise description of the general method to guide their understanding. With a readable program and a few well-chosen examples it is much easier to learn the skills. Such intellectual skills are very hard to transfer without the medium of computer programming. Indeed, "a computer language is not just a way of getting a computer to perform operations but rather it is a novel formal medium for expressing ideas about methodology. Thus programs must be written for people to read, and only incidentally for machines to execute" (Abelson et al., *Structure and Interpretation of Computer Programs*, 1996).

I have used computational descriptions to communicate methodological ideas in teaching subjects in electrical circuits and in signals and systems. Jack Wisdom and I have written a book and are teaching a class that uses computational techniques to communicate a deeper understanding of classical mechanics. Our class is targeted for advanced undergraduates and graduate students in physics and engineering. In our class computational algorithms are used to express the methods used in the analysis of dynamical phenomena. Expressing the methods in a computer language forces them to be unambiguous and computationally effective. Students are expected to read our programs and to extend them and to write new ones. The task of formulating a method as a computer-executable program and debugging that program is a powerful exercise in the learning process. Also, once formalized procedurally, a mathematical idea becomes a tool that can be used directly to compute results.

We may think that teaching engineering and science is quite removed from daily culture, but this is wrong. Back in 1980 (a long time ago!) I was walking around an exhibit of primitive personal computers at a trade show. I passed a station where a small girl (perhaps 9 years old) was typing furiously at a computer. While I watched, she reached over to a man standing nearby and pulled on his sleeve and said: "Daddy! Daddy! This computer is very smart. Its BASIC knows about recursive definitions!" I am sure that her father had no idea what she was talking about. But notice: the idea of a recursive definition was only a mathematician's dream in the 1930s. It was advanced computer science in the 1950s and 1960s. By 1980 a little girl had a deep enough operational understanding of the idea to construct an effective test and to appreciate its significance.

At this moment in history we are only at the beginning of an intellectual revolution based on the assimilation of computational ideas. The previous revolutions took a long time for the consequences to actualize. It is hard to predict where this one will lead. I see one of the deepest consequences of computational thinking entering our society in the transformation of our view of ourselves. Previous revolutions have entered culture by affecting the way we think and the way we talk: we discuss economic phenomena in terms of "market forces." We talk about geopolitical developments as having "momentum." We think it is hard to accomplish an organizational change because of "inertia." In exactly the same way we will find computational metaphors sneaking into our vocabulary. We already hear ourselves describing some social interactions as "networking." We may "ping" a friend to see if he "acks," indicating that he is available. But these are still rather superficial. More telling is the fact that we can describe people and organizations as having "bugs," and that these can be "patched." Perhaps the most important consequence of computational thinking will be in the development of an understanding of ourselves as computational beings. Indeed, my personal experience as a computer programmer has made me aware that many of my own problems are bugs that can be analyzed and debugged, often with great effort, and sometimes patched.

FAIRY TALES

Allen Newell, Carnegie Mellon University

NOTE: This essay is reprinted by permission of
Allen Newell Archives, Carnegie Mellon University.
Presented September 17, 1976,
at an inaugural party for the establishment of the
U.A. and Helen Whitaker Professorships
at Carnegie Mellon University,
it appeared originally in *FOCUS*, December 1976.

Once upon a time, when it was still of some use to wish for what one wanted, . . .

> . . . there lived a King and Queen who had a daughter who was lovely to behold, but who never laughed.

Or perhaps:

> . . . there lived an old fisherman by the side of a sea that had hardly any fishes in it.

If you are like me, you are already hooked. You are ready to abandon all talk of computers and electronic technology and professorships, and settle in to hear a fairy story. Their attraction reaches almost all of us.

They let us enter in upon an enchanted world. Magic abounds, though always in special ways. Animals talk, and not only animals but trees and bridges. Villainy is there, certainly danger. There are trials to be overcome—usually three of them. But there is always the happy ending. The spell is broken and the Princess smiles and marries the youth who made her laugh. The old fisherman gets the Jinni back in the bottle with the top on. And happiness is ever after, which means at least for a little while.

The experts tell us that fairy tales are for childhood. That they contain lessons for the crises of growing up, and that their universal attraction comes because they deal with what is central to this universal time of life:

Like Hansel and Gretel, we have to leave home and find our own way.

Like Jack, in the story of the beanstalk, we can bring home the bacon if we persevere, even if our parents don't think we can.

But there was more, if you remember your Jack. First he escaped back home with a bag of gold. But Jack and his mother used up the gold, showing that one success is not enough.

Then he made a second trip up the beanstalk to the Giant's castle. This time he came home with the magic hen that lays golden eggs, so he now had a technology for satisfying his and his mother's wants.

But even so, material things are not sufficient for the full life. So on his third trip Jack brought home the golden singing harp, symbolizing the higher things of life.

Or like the Princess with the Frog King, we must learn to keep our word and embrace what we find ugly and disgusting, to discover that it contains our heart's desire.

The experts notwithstanding, fairy stories are for all of us. Indeed, this is true if for no other reason than that today we are all of us children with respect to the future. We do not know what is coming. It is as new and as incomprehensible as adult life is to children. We find ourselves troubled and fearful at the changes taking place in ourselves and our society. We need the hidden guidance of fairy stories to tell us of the trials we must overcome. To assure us that there will be a happy ending. Whether fairy stories have been written that speak to the heart of our own adult crises is unclear. How would we, the children, ever know? Perhaps we must get along with the fairy stories we have. We could do worse.

But even more, fairy stories seem to me to have a close connection to technology. That the aim of technology, when properly applied, is to build a land of Faerie.

Well, that should come as a shock! The intellectual garb of the modern academic is cynicism. Like a follower in a great herd, as surely as I am an academic, I am a cynic. Yet, I have just uttered a sentiment that is, if anything, straight from Pollyanna.

In point of fact, within the small circle of writers who manage to put technology and fairy stories between the same covers, the emphasis is always on the negative, on the dark side. The favorite stories are those that trouble.

Like the Sorcerer's Apprentice, who learns only enough magic to start the broom of technology hauling water from the River Rhine to the cistern, but who cannot stop it.

Like the Jinni in the bottle, where the story is never permitted to go to the conclusion in the Arabian Nights, with the Jinni snookered back into the bottle, but is always stopped with the Jinni hanging in air and the question along with it—Can we ever put the Jinni back? Or will there only be ink all over the sky 'til the stars go out?

Like the many stories of the three magic wishes, in which, promising infinite riches just for the asking, they are always spent, first on foolishness, second on disaster, and third on bare recovery. As in the Monkey's Paw, the old couple's first wish was for just 200 pounds. That was foolish. The second wish was for the return of their just killed son. That was disaster. The third wish was to send their son back to his opened grave to try to recover for themselves a world where life could go on.

But I see it differently. I see the computer as the enchanted technology. Better, it is the technology of enchantment. I mean that quite literally, so I had best explain.

There are two essential ingredients in computer technology. First, it is the technology of how to apply knowledge to action to achieve goals. That is, it provides the capability for intelligent behavior. That is why we process data with computers—to get answers to solve our problems. That is what algorithms and programs are all about—frozen action to be thawed when needed.

The second ingredient is the miniaturization of the physical systems that have this ability for intelligent action. This is what Angel Jordan, my co-Whitaker Professor, has been telling us about. Computers are getting smaller, and cheaper, and faster, and more reliable, and less energy demanding. Everything is changing in the right direction together. The good things do not trade off against the bad ones. More speed does not mean more dollars. Smaller size does not mean lower reliability. On any given date, these tradeoffs that the economists so dearly love, of having to choose between painful options, clearly do hold. But come back next year and everything is better: smaller, cheaper, faster, more reliable, and for less energy.

Thus computer technology differs from all other technologies precisely in providing the capability for an enchanted world:

For brakes that know how to stop on wet pavement.

For instruments that can converse with their users.

For bridges that watch out for the safety of those who cross them.

For streetlights that care about those who stand under them—who know the way, so no one need get lost.

For little boxes that make out your income tax for you.

In short, computer technology offers the possibility of incorporating intelligent behavior in all the nooks and crannies of our world. With it we could build an enchanted land.

All very good. What about the Sorcerer's Apprentice? That comes about because of two half-fallacies. The first half-fallacy is that technologies are rigid and unthinking. Start the broom off carrying water and it does that and not something else. But every computer scientist recognizes in the Sorcerer's Apprentice simply a program with a bug in it, embedded in a first generation operation system with no built in panic button. Even with our computer systems today, poor things as they are, such blunderbuss looping is no longer a specter.

Exactly what the computer provides is the ability to not be rigid and unthinking, but rather to behave conditionally. That is what it means to apply knowledge to action: it means to let the action taken reflect knowledge of the situation, to be sometimes this way, sometimes that, as appropriate. With small amounts of computer technology—that is, with small amounts of memory and small amounts of processing per decision—you often can't be conditional enough. That is certainly the story of the first decades of the computer revolution. It was too expensive and involved too much complexity to create systems with enough conditionality. We didn't know how and couldn't have afforded it if we had. Consequently, many applications were rigid and unthinking. It was indeed a Sorcerer's Apprentice who seemed to run the computerized billing service.

However, the import of miniaturization is that ultimately, we will be able to have enough capability for conditionality in a small enough space. And the import of our scientific study of computers is that we will know how to make all the conditionality work for us. Then the brooms of the world themselves can know enough to stop when things go wrong.

The second half-fallacy behind the Sorcerer's Apprentice is that technologies by their nature extract too high a price. That is a message of the recent literature of political ecology. Our technologies inevitably demand that we use up our precious world. There is rather abundant evidence for this view. Here in Western Pennsylvania, the price to the enchantment of our countryside for taking our coal by strip mining is only too much in evidence. Less in our awareness, because it was so thorough, was what the loggers did to Western Pennsylvania. Not once, but thrice, within forty years they swept the hillsides almost bare. The hot scalding breath of a dragon could hardly have done better for desolation.

But all is not inevitable. Ecologically, computer technology itself is nearly magic. The better it gets, the less of our environment it consumes. It is clean, unobtrusive, consumes little energy and little material. And as we push it to higher peaks of speed and memory, it becomes more of all these things. For deep technical reasons this has to be. There is no way to obtain immense amounts of processing power by freezing technology at some cost in dollars, material, and energy per unit of computation, and then just buying more and more of it, consuming our wealth and our environment. Instead, for a long time to come, as we get more and more of it, the less it will impact our environment.

Even more, the computer is exactly the technology to permit us to cope intelligently with the use of our other resources. Again, by providing us with distributed intelligence, it can let us keep track of the use and abuse of our environment. And not only of the destruction that we ourselves visit on our world, but also that which nature does as well. Mt. Vesuvius was hardly bound by any antipollution ordinances posted on the walls of ancient Pompeii.

In sum, technology can be controlled, especially if it is saturated with intelligence to watch over how it goes, to keep accounts, to prevent errors, and to provide wisdom to each decision. And these guardians of our world, these magic informational dwarfs, need not extract too high a price.

But I said that the Sorcerer's Apprentice was guided by *half-fallacies.* I did not dismiss the view totally. Because, of course, in fairy stories there are great trials to be performed before the happy ending. Great dangers must be encountered and overcome. Because also, in fairy stories, the hero—the one who achieves finally the happy ending (and it is as often a girl-child as a boy-child)—must grow in virtue and in mature understanding. No villains need apply for the central role. The fairy story that I am indirectly spinning here will not come automatically and we must earn it.

Where are we now? We are not at the end of the story, though we are surely at the end of my talk. In fact, the fairy story is hardly past its "Once upon a time." Still, I wish to assert that computer science and technology are the stuff out of which the future fairy land can be built. My faith is that the trials can be endured successfully, even by us children who fear that we are not so wise as we need to be. I might remind you, by the way, that the hero never has to make it all on his own. Prometheus is not the central character of any fairy story but of a tragic myth. In fairy stories, magic friends sustain our hero and help him overcome the giants and the witches that beset him.

Finally, I wish to express my feeling of childlike wonder that my time to be awake on this earth has placed me in the middle of this particular fairy story.

REVISITING "WHAT IS COMPUTER SCIENCE"

Allen Newell, Carnegie Mellon University

NOTE: Reprinted by permission of
Allen Newell Archives, Carnegie Mellon University.

As the enterprise of science matures, the universe gets parceled out to different sciences and disciplines—physics, chemistry, biology, psychology, history, the arts, engineering, etc. This organization is not static. Refinements occur, so psychology becomes cognitive, social and developmental psychology. Boundaries enlarge, so biology and chemistry produce biochemistry. Reorganizations occur, so the anatomy, physiology and pharmacology of the brain form into neuroscience. After a while brand new sciences rarely emerge, despite the restless jostling, because the existing disciplines, though a patchwork, cover all that mankind believes exists at a given moment in history. It requires the emergence of something quite unexpected. The discovery of micro-organisms, leading to microbiology, and genes, leading to genetics—both events in the nineteenth century provide examples.

Computer science has been such an event. Its emergence has been especially confusing because of the computer's origin as an engineered and manufactured device. As one wag put it, if there is a science of computers then why not a science of washing machines? Back in the 1960s, just as the first departments of computer science were forming, there was a fair amount of such questioning, especially by members of the well-established disciplines such as physics and mathematics. In response to that climate, Herb Simon, Alan Perlis and myself wrote a letter to the editors in *Science*, the journal of the American Association for the Advancement of Science, which was (and still is) the journal with the largest reach into the entire scientific establishment. That letter is reproduced on the following pages and speaks for itself.

It is good to have an opportunity to reprint the letter. It is rare that I would not change an iota of something I have helped author. This letter is such a case. It still says exactly what I want to say about the nature of computer science. My co-authors felt the same way, I'm sure. Alan actually recorded his assessment. In his talk at the tenth anniversary of [Carnegie Mellon's] Computer Science [Department], he said:

> Some years back in the publication that I hope my name will be bound most closely to, Herb Simon, Al Newell, and I submitted a letter to *Science* Magazine in which we said what computer science was. And in our confessed ignorance, we said it had to be the study of the phenomena

arising around computers. We were right then, we're right today, and I think we'll be right twenty years from now. The computer should make us all humble because it is not possible for any of us, no matter how bright we are, or what our experience, to predict what it is going to be used for. It may ultimately disappear and be hidden under all kinds of gadgets and never be seen again, like the electric motor, and our only memories of the computer will be abstractions—things we talk about, things we draw, music we play. Who knows? But to say that computer science is artificial intelligence, or complexity theory, or programming languages, or operating systems or what-not, is ridiculous.[1]

The response of the field has not been so uniformly positive. Many occasions arise to enunciate the essential nature of computer science. The letter almost always gets evoked as one possibility. Almost invariably, it is set aside in favor of something that seems to be more elegant or more conceptually integrative. The preferred candidate usually has a strong flavor of computer science being the study of algorithms. However important algorithms are—and they are indeed important—much of the richness of computer science would disappear if we really took the central task to be discovering algorithms and understanding their nature. Fortunately, in accord with Objection 3 of the letter, living computers spark off new phenomena at a high enough rate to stay ahead of any of the attempts to characterize the field in terms of some partial view, however insightful.

What Is Computer Science[2]

Allen Newell, Alan Perlis, Herbert Simon

Professors of computer science are often asked: "Is there such a thing as computer science, and if there is, what is it?" The questions have a simple answer:

Whenever there are phenomena, there can be a science to describe and explain those phenomena. Thus, the simplest (and correct) answer to "What is botany?" is, "Botany is the study of plants." And zoology is the

---

[1]Appeared in *Perspectives on Computer Science: From the 10th Anniversary Symposium at the Computer Science Department, Carnegie Mellon University,* Anita K. Jones (ed.), Academic Press, 1977, Keynote Speech, p. 2.

[2]This letter appeared in *Science*, Vol. 157, No. 3795, September 22, 1967, pp. 1373-1374. Permission was granted for use of the letter as it appeared in the *Computer Science Research Review*, S. Dewald (ed.), Computation Center and Department of Computer Science, Carnegie Mellon University, 1967.

study of animals, astronomy the study of stars, and so on. Phenomena breed sciences.

There are computers. Ergo, *computer science is the study of computers.* The phenomena surrounding computers are varied, complex, rich. It remains only to answer the objections.

Objection 1. Only natural phenomena breed sciences, but computers are artificial, hence are whatever they are made to be, hence obey no invariable laws, hence cannot be described and explained.

— *Answer.* 1. The objection is patently false, since computers and computer programs are being described and explained daily. 2. The objection would equally rule out of science large portions of organic chemistry (substitute "silicones" for "computers"), physics (substitute "superconductivity" for "computers") and even botany, (substitute "hybrid corn" for "computers"). The objection would certainly rule out mathematics, but in any event its status as a natural science is idiosyncratic.

Objection 2. The term "computer" is not well defined, and its meaning will change with new developments; hence computer science does not have a well-defined subject matter.

— *Answer.* The phenomena of all sciences change over time; the process of understanding assures that this will be the case. Astronomy did not originally include the study of interstellar gases; physics did not include radioactivity; psychology did not include the study of animal behavior. Mathematics was once defined as the "science of quantity."

Objection 3. Computer science is the study of algorithms (or programs), not computers.

— *Answer.* 1. Showing deeper insight than they are sometimes credited with, the founders of the chief professional organization for computer science named it the Association for Computing Machinery. 2. In the definition "computers" means "living computers"—i.e., the hardware, their programs or algorithms, and all that goes with them. Computer science is the study of the phenomena surrounding computers. "Computers plus algorithms," "living computers," or simply "computers" all come to the same thing—the same phenomena.

Objection 4. Computers, like thermometers, are instruments, not phenomena. Instruments lead away to their user sciences; the behaviors of instruments are subsumed as special topics in other sciences (not always the user sciences—electron microscopy belongs to physics, not biology).

— *Answer.* The computer is such a novel and complex instrument that its behavior is subsumed under no other science; its study does not lead away to user sciences, but to further study of computers. Hence, the computer is not *just* an instrument but a phenomenon as well, requiring description and explanation.

Objection 5. Computer science is a branch of electronics (or mathematics, psychology, etc.).

— *Answer.* To study computers, one may need to study some or all of these. Phenomena define the focus of a science, not its boundaries. Many of the phenomena of computers are also phenomena of some other science. The existence of biochemistry denies the existence of neither biology nor chemistry. But all of the phenomena of computers are not subsumed under any one existing science.

Objection 6. Computers belong to engineering, not science.

— *Answer.* They belong to both, like electricity (physics and electrical engineering) or plants (botany and agriculture). Time will tell what professional specialization is desirable between analysis and synthesis, and between the pure study of computers and their applications.

Computer scientists will often join hands with colleagues from other disciplines in a common endeavor. Mostly, computer scientists will study living computers with the same passion that others have studied plants, stars, glaciers, dyestuffs, and magnetism; and with the same confidence that intelligent, persistent curiosity will yield interesting and perhaps useful knowledge.

Some Computer Scientists at
Carnegie Mellon University
Pittsburgh, Pennsylvania
Allen Newell
Alan J. Perlis
Herbert A. Simon

Appendix

Agenda of July 25-26, 2001, Symposium

WEDNESDAY, JULY 25, 2001

1:30 p.m.   **Opening Remarks**

Mary Shaw, Carnegie Mellon University, and Chair, Committee on the Fundamentals of Computer Science

1:45 - 3:15   **Session 1: Impacts of Computer Science**

Edward L. Ayers, University of Virginia—*Understanding the Past as Information*
Susan Landau, Sun Microsystems—*The Profound Effect of CS on the Practice and Teaching of Mathematics*
Michael Lesk, National Science Foundation—*Computer Science Is to Information as Chemistry Is to Matter*

3:15 - 3:30   **Break**

3:30 - 4:00   **Guest Speaker**

William A. Wulf, National Academy of Engineering—*The Engineering and Science Fundamentals of Computer Science*

4:00 - 5:30   **Session 2: Sampling of Hard Research Questions in Computer Science**

Sriram Rajamani, Microsoft Research—*Specifying and Checking Properties of Programs*
Lillian Lee, Cornell University—*"I'm Sorry Dave, I'm Afraid I Can't Do That": Linguistics, Statistics, and Natural Language Processing in 2001*
Chee Yap, New York University—*Toward Robust Geometric Computation*

5:30   **Reception**

6:30 p.m.   **Dinner**

THURSDAY, JULY 26, 2001

7:30 a.m.   **Continental Breakfast**

8:30 - 10:30   **Session 3: CS Research: Content and Character**

Ursula Martin, University of St. Andrews—*What Is Computer Science?—The European Perspective*
Neil Immerman, University of Massachusetts, Amherst—*On the Unusual Effectiveness of Logic in Computer Science*
Amy Bruckman, Georgia Institute of Technology—*Synergies Between Educational Theory and Computer Science*
Gerald Sussman, Massachusetts Institute of Technology—*The Legacy of Computer Science*

10:30 - 10:45   **Break**

10:45 - 12:00   **Wrap-up Discussion—What Makes Computer Science Vital and Exciting?**

All-participant discussion, moderated by Jim Foley, Georgia Institute of Technology